SELECTED POEMS OF ANNA AKHMATOVA

SELECTED POEMS OF
ANNA AKHMATOVA

TRANSLATED BY

JUDITH HEMSCHEMEYER

EDITED & INTRODUCED BY

ROBERTA REEDER

ZEPHYR PRESS

BROOKLINE, MASSACHUSETTS

First Printing, November 2000

ISBN 0-939010-61-5
Library of Congress Control Number: 00-136016

The paper used in this book meets the minimum requirements of the American National Standard of Permanence of Paper for Printed Library Materials Z39.48-1984.

ZEPHYR PRESS
50 Kenwood Street
Brookline, Massachusetts
02446, U.S.A.

www.zephyrpress.org

Acknowledgement is gratefully made to the following periodicals, in which some of these translations initially appeared: *Agni Review, Boulevard, Calyx, Frank* (Paris), *Gargoyle* (Washington, D.C.), *Green House, The Hudson Review, I/Q: International Quarterly, Kalliope, Mundus Artium, The Nantucket Review, New England Review and Bread Loaf Quarterly, New Letters, Northwest Review, Pequod, Ploughshares, Poetry Now, Prism International* (University of British Columbia, Canada), *rara avis, Room, Southern Review* (University of Adelaide, Australia), *The SouthernReview, Stand, TriQuarterly.*

Book and cover design
by *typeslowly*

Cover print of Akhmatova
by Stephen Alcorn

Text set in Slimbach's Minion
and Minion Cyrillic

Book printed in Michigan
by Cushing-Malloy, Inc.

Table of Contents

from *WHITE FLOCK*

from *PLANTAIN*

from *ANNO DOMINI MCMXXI*

from *REED*

from *SEVENTH BOOK*

from *ODD NUMBER*

UNCOLLECTED POEMS AND FRAGMENTS

1904–1917

1919–1941

1941–MAY 1945

SEPTEMBER 1945–1956

1957–1966

Publisher's Note

Poems in this collection were selected by Judith Hemschemeyer from *The Complete Poems of Anna Akhmatova*, also available from Zephyr Press. Roberta Reeder, editor of that book, suggested a number of additional poems. The full range of the poet's career is represented here, with the exception of "Poem Without a Hero." We hope to be able to issue a comprehensive bilingual edition of "Poem Without a Hero" as a companion to this book.

A few typographical errors have been corrected; otherwise the text of the poems has not been altered from the Expanded Third Edition (1997) of *The Complete Poems*. Some scholarly references have been edited out of the notes for this publication; these can be consulted intact in *The Complete Poems*, as can the full text of the translator's introduction, which is excerpted here.

Many readers new to Akhmatova's poetry are uncertain how to pronounce her name. The accent falls on the second syllable. (And for those who enjoy reading aloud, the river that runs through St. Petersburg and Akhmatova's verse, the Neva, is also accented on the second syllable.)

With each new edition of the poems of Anna Akhmatova, the list of acknowledgments of those who help to keep her work in print grows longer. In addition to those already acknowledged in *The Complete Poems of Anna Akhmatova*, we would like to thank David and Linda Blair, Tatiana Elisavetskaya, Adrian Flatgard, John Fraser, Jean Kates, the Kates Foundation, Kathy Lu, Tatiana Malysheva, Charles Merrill Jr., Jane Pincus, Inna Poluyanova, Vladimir Popov (of the FTM Agency in Moscow), Alfia Rakova, Eduard Safronsky, the Tiny Tiger Foundation, Howard Zaharoff and Natalia Zhidkova for their contributions and support.

Translator's Preface

Judith Hemschemeyer

In 1973 I read a few of Anna Akhmatova's poems in translation in the *American Poetry Review* and was so struck by one of them that I decided to learn Russian in order to read them all. Here is the poem, from *White Flock,* Akhmatova's third book:

The sky's dark blue lacquer has dimmed,
And louder the song of the ocarina.
It's only a little pipe of clay,
There's no reason for it to complain.
Who told it all my sins,
And why is it absolving me?...
Or is this a voice repeating
Your latest poems to me?

Three years later, when I could read the Russian and compare the existing, "selected Akhmatova" translations with the originals, I became convinced that Akhmatova's poems should be translated in their entirety, and by a woman poet, and that I was that person. Using literals provided by Ann Wilkinson for the first 300 poems and by Natasha Gurfinkel and Roberta Reeder for the rest, I translated the poems in the order established by the Formalist critic Viktor Zhirmunsky in the Biblioteka Poeta edition of Akhmatova's works, published in Leningrad in 1976. Zhirmunsky reproduced Akhmatova's five early, uncensored books — *Evening* (1912), *Rosary* (1914), *White Flock* (1917), *Plantain* (1921), and *Anno Domini MCMXXI* (1922) — in the order in which they were published. Just as important, he retained the poet's ordering of the poems within each volume; this allows us to participate in Akhmatova's life and loves as she orchestrated them.

The act of translating, as anyone who has tried it will attest, entails sacrifices. For the music and the delicious web of connotations of the original one substitutes, if one is lucky and patient, a verbal equivalent that conveys the tone and the meaning and some kind of music of its own. The music of a translation is not the original music, of course. My suggestion is that the English-speaking reader find a Russian friend to read aloud (or recite, as many Russians will be able to do) some of the poems and thus gain some idea of the rich texture of sounds and the driving rhythms that Akhmatova achieves.

My first goal was to understand the poem; only then, I felt, could I present the poem to others. This took time — more than ten years — and at least several versions of each poem.

Because the Russian language has six cases, it is extremely rich in full rhymes, while English is extremely poor. To illustrate: how many words in English rhyme with father? The word father in Russian is, depending on its case, pronounced *ot-yets, ot-sa, ot-su, ot-se* or *ot-som.* The plural endings present another set of rhyming possibilities. Thus in Russian almost any noun can be made to rhyme with any other noun. Adjectives, too, are declined — even the numbers — and verbs are conjugated; this enriches the chance for rhyming as well. Word order in the English sentence is fairly rigid, but the case endings in Russian allow for all sorts of flexibility, hence still more rhyming possibilities.

A typical lyric of Akhmatova's was 12 or 16 lines, three or four stanzas, rhymed a-b-a-b, c-d-c-d, etc. To reproduce this as full rhyme in English, one would have to skew the sense of the poem by reaching for a rhyming word at the expense of the meaning. And the result would be a trite-sounding series of jingles whose rhymes are boringly anticipated by the reader, a sort of doggerel.

I chose instead to utilize the occasional full rhyme that occurred, but to rely mainly on slant rhyme, internal rhyme, assonance and alliteration to construct the poem in English. What I found myself producing as the work went on was often an x-a-y-a rhyme scheme, one that satisfies but doesn't cloy the ear.

As for rhythm — the Russian language has a wealth of magnificent polysyllabic words and since each word gets only one accent, the good poet can command a healthy variation of metrical feet in the line. Akhmatova was a master of prosody. She used an exceptionally high number of amphibrachs — an unaccented syllable, an accented syllable, then another unaccented syllable — with the effect of suggesting rising and falling, tension and release. It was, of course, impossible to adhere to Akhmatova's exact meters and say in English what has to be said. But I repeated the poem over and over to myself in Russian to get the rhythm. Then, using the literal translation as a base, I would invite felicitous English words to alight in some kind of regular line.

I was very careful to retain Akhmatova's verbs and Akhmatova's images and I found, I think, an equivalent for her diction, which is direct but not slangy, precise but never precious. I did not add lines of explication in the body of the poem; endnotes take care of that. I also tried, as far as possible, to keep Akhmatova's line breaks and the look of the poem on the page.

Here is a sonnet Akhmatova wrote in 1962, remembering the visit Isaiah Berlin paid to her. Her sonnet rhymes a-b-a-b, c-d-c-d, e-e-f,g-g-f and has lines of 10 and 9 syllables. My translation rhymes a-b-b-a,c-d-d-c,b-e-e, f-g-g. Some of my rhymes are direct, some are slant rhymes.

I abandoned your shores, Empress,
against my will.
— Aeneid, Book 6

Don't be afraid — I can still portray
What we resemble now.
You are a ghost — or a man passing through,
And for some reason I cherish your shade.
For awhile you were my Aeneas —
It was then I escaped by fire.
We know how to keep quiet about one another.
And you forgot my cursed house.

You forgot those hands stretched out to you
In horror and torment, through flame,
And the report of blasted dreams.

You don't know for what you were forgiven...
Rome was created, flocks of flotillas sail on the sea,
And adulation sings the praises of victory.

Although I aimed for a basic decasyllabic line, I also wanted to have the meaning of each line in English match its Russian counterpart. Consequently, line 2 has only 6 syllables and there are other lines of 13 or 14 syllables. Still, it is a recognizable sonnet and it says, as gracefully as I found possible, what Akhmatova's sonnet says.

Each poem presented a new puzzle; many defied the rough formula I had devised of rhyming the second and fourth line of Akhmatova's quatrain. In this poem, for example, the end rhymes are a-b-a-b, c-d-c-d, e-f-e-f in Russian.

THE LAST ONE

I delighted in deliriums,
In singing about tombs.
I distributed misfortunes
Beyond anyone's strength.
The curtain not raised,
The circle dance of shades —
Because of that, all my loved ones
Were taken away.
All this is disclosed
In the depths of the roses.
But I am not allowed to forget
The taste of the tears of yesterday.

What I have managed to devise and still stay faithful to the meaning and the line breaks is the consonance of "deliriums" and "tombs," the assonance of "deliriums" and "misfortunes," the alliteration of "delighted," "deliriums" and "distributed," the rhyming of "disclosed" and rose" and the five long *a* sounds that, because they are so strong in English, provide the poem's dominant musical chord: "raised," "shades," "away," "taste" and "yesterday."

Because of the high achievement of Akhmatova's poetry, I never begrudged the hours and years of labor it took to solve these puzzles, these poems, one after the other. What emerges from my efforts are, I hope, translations that will give the reader of English some idea of the intensity with which Akhmatova lived and wrote.

As time elapsed, I learned about her not only through her poems, but through the writings of her contemporaries, and the more I learned, the more I admired her courage, her moral integrity, her wit and, yes, her sense of humor under the direst of circumstances. Nadezhda Mandelstam has this to say about Akhmatova's character in *Hope Abandoned*:

> One way or another I expect I shall now live out my life to the end, spurred on by the memory of Akhmatova's Russian powers of endurance; it was her boast to have so exasperated the accusers who had denounced her and her poetry that they all died before her of heart attacks.

Judith Hemschemeyer

Mirrors and Masks: The Life and Poetic Works of Anna Akhmatova

Roberta Reeder

A POET'S LIFE CAN BE REFLECTED IN MANY MIRRORS. The life of Anna Akhmatova has been reflected in autobiographical notes, recorded conversations, letters and diaries of contemporaries, and criticism of her works. Yet she remains mysterious in many ways. She was discreet about the events in her personal life, and restrained in expression. Though often inspired by real events or emotions, her poems may mask more than they reveal. Akhmatova warned against scrutinizing her lyrics for insight into her thoughts and feelings: "Lyric verse is the best armor, the best cover. You don't give yourself away."[1]

Akhmatova practiced her art under extraordinarily difficult conditions in one of the most complex epochs of Russian history. Despite the hardships she endured, Akhmatova never expressed self-pity; instead she transformed personal pain and the tragedies of her nation into transcendent and immortal lyrics: "I never stopped writing poems. In them is my link with time, with the new life of my people. When I wrote them, I believed in the resounding rhythms reflected in the heroic history of my country. I am happy that I lived in these years and saw events which cannot be equalled."[2]

Early Years: 1889–1914

Akhmatova was born in a time of chaos and ferment. The revolution was slow in coming, but increasingly violent and radical political outbursts heralded its arrival. As the end of the Romanov dynasty and the twilight of Imperial Russia drew near,[3] Tsar Nicholas II, a notoriously weak and indecisive ruler, made frantic efforts to preserve the foundations of a crumbling monarchy.

She was born Anna Gorenko on 23 June 1889 (11 June, Old Style)[4] in Bolshoy Fontan on the Black Sea, near Odessa, in the Ukraine. Her father was Ukrainian[5] and her mother of Russian origin. Akhmatova's family moved north to the town of Pavlovsk and soon after to Tsarskoye Selo, near St. Petersburg, when she was eleven months old. She grew up there amidst elegant pavilions, allées lined with tall trees, and beautiful parks with replicas of ancient statues. She was deeply affected by the presence of Alexander Pushkin, the great Russian poet, who had attended the Tsarskoye Selo lyceum for sons of the nobility.

As a child, Akhmatova heard the sounds of the Russian poet Nikolay Nekrasov, whose verses were full of sympathy for the plight of the lower classes. Her mother, who had been active in politics in her youth, recited his poems to her.[6] Nekrasov's descriptions of the Russian landscape influenced Akhmatova's own poetry. His works presented Akhmatova with examples of Russian women of all classes who were oppressed, but who displayed a fortitude that Akhmatova later displayed in both her life and work.

She was also deeply affected by the catastrophic and embarrassing defeat of the Russian fleet in 1905 in the straits of Tsushima during the Russo-Japanese War which marked a major turning point in Russian history. According to her memoirs, she began writing poetry in 1900 although, as she freely admitted, her early verses were very poor.

By 1911, she was publishing under the name of Anna Akhmatova. Her pseudonym, Akhmatova, came from the family name of her maternal great-grandmother, and of the last Tatar princes from the Horde.[7] The impetus for the name change, according to Akhmatova, was her father. When he found out that she was writing poetry, he commanded her not to "bring shame upon [the family] name."[8]

In 1906, Akhmatova returned to Kiev to complete her last year of studies at the Fundukleyevskaya Gymnaziya. She joined the Faculty of Law at the Kiev College for Women in the autumn of 1907, but soon grew bored. At this time, her letters reflect her unhappy state, as she compares herself to Cassandra: "I have murdered my soul, and my eyes are created for tears, as Iolanthe says. Or do you remember Schiller's prophetic Cassandra? One facet of my soul adjoins the dark image of this prophetess, so great in her suffering. But I am far from greatness."[9]

In letters written between 1906 and 1907, Akhmatova reveals her ambivalence about the young poet, Nikolay Gumilyov, who was ardently pursuing her. They had met in 1903 while attending school. Valeriya Sreznevskaya describes him at this time, noting he was not very handsome and was somewhat wooden, arrogant and insecure; nonetheless, he had a certain elegance.[10]

Despite her professed indifference to him, Akhmatova married Gumilyov on 25 April 1910, in a church near Kiev, believing him to be her "destiny." Gumilyov was the first to publish Akhmatova's poems, in his journal *Sirius* in 1907. He himself had already published two collections of poems, *The Path of the Conquistadors,* and *Romantic flowers,* both heavily influenced by the French Symbolists.[11] In his poetry Gumilyov saw himself as a conquistador and in fact journeyed abroad in quest of the unknown; he made frequent trips to Africa, starting in 1907.[12]

The couple spent their honeymoon in Paris. In September 1910, Gumilyov left his young bride for another African expedition. While he was away, Akhmatova attended Professor Rayev's courses on the History of Literature.[13]

In the spring of 1911, Akhmatova spent several weeks in Paris alone, and formed a close friendship with the Italian painter Amedeo Modigliani. She and Gumilyov settled in Tsarskoye Selo in his family home and spent summers in Slepnyovo on his mother's estate in Tver province. However, Gumilyov's trips abroad and constant desire to seek adventure elsewhere dominated their marriage and helped destroy it.

In Petersburg, the flourishing literary scene was dominated by the Symbolists.[14] Practitioners of Symbolism, who viewed the poet as the bearer of a spiritual message rather than as a social reformer, began to interpret the impending revolution as an apocalyptic event that would purge Russia of all corruption and sin. Alexander

Blok, a key Symbolist figure, was one of Akhmatova's greatest influences. Rather than a continuation of his work, hers was a conscious reaction against it; however, some of her poems show traces of Symbolism with its love of fantasy, costume, and the eighteenth century. Later in her career, Akhmatova paid homage to the importance of Symbolism: "The modernists did a great thing for Russia. They taught people to love verse again."[15]

Meanwhile Akhmatova was becoming a leading figure in the artistic world of Petersburg. She developed from a shy, young girl to a self-assured, regal woman in only a few years. Many poets and other members of the intelligentsia gathered in the apartment of Vyacheslav Ivanov, known as "The Tower." There, in the spring of 1911, Akhmatova first met another young poet, Osip Mandelstam.

Another site at which the various artistic and cultural currents converged, met, and clashed was the cellar cabaret, the Stray Dog, which opened on 31 December 1911. The central figure of the cabaret was actress, dancer and singer Olga Glebova-Sudeikina. Poets who recited at the cabaret included Akhmatova, Mikhail Kuzmin, Mandelstam, and Vladimir Mayakovsky, a member of the Futurist movement, which rejected all art of the past and embraced the age of Modernism and technology. Another frequent participant in the Stray Dog events was avant-garde composer Artur Lourié, who, inspired by the broad freedoms initially granted to artists, served as the first Soviet Commissar of Music. He had a brief affair with Akhmatova in 1913.[16]

In 1911, Gumilyov played a leading role in forming the Poets' Guild, following his break with Ivanov.[17] Six of its members — Gumilyov, Akhmatova, Gorodetsky, Mandelstam, Vladimir Narbut, and Mikhail Zenkevich — founded Acmeism, a movement that rejected the mysticism and ornate style of Symbolism. By the time Akhmatova published her first collection, *Evening*, in 1912, the Symbolist movement was in crisis. In a pivotal article called "Overcoming Symbolism" (1916), critic Viktor Zhirmunsky asserted that Akhmatova, Gumilyov and Mandelstam had transcended the Symbolist aesthetic.

Akhmatova published forty-six poems in *Evening*. The 300 copies sold out quickly. Mikhail Kuzmin, who wrote the preface, went so far as to assert that the appearance of *Evening* marked a dramatic turn in Russian poetry.[18] The eminent writer and critic Korney Chukovsky observed that the youth of two or three generations fell in love to the accompaniment of Akhmatova's poetry.[19]

Evening concentrates on the many facets of love, from awakening hope to joyful fulfillment, from disillusionment to the last embers of a dying relationship. Her verse is distinguished by its sparseness and its restraint, in sharp contrast to the more extravagant Symbolist verse.

These poems are not necessarily autobiographical self-portraits. The poet takes on a broad range of personas, from a peasant woman beaten by her husband to an elegant member of the upper class; in rare instances, there is a male speaker.

In September 1912, soon after *Evening*'s publication, Akhmatova gave birth to a son, Lev Gumilyov; nevertheless, there were indications that both Akhmatova and Gumilyov were growing disillusioned with their marriage.[20] There are conflicting accounts about Akhmatova's attitude toward motherhood: Sreznevskaya claims that the birth made Akhmatova feel confined,[21] while Pavel Luknitsky attests to her having had strong maternal instincts which began to dissipate only after Gumilyov's family took the child, against Akhmatova's wishes.[22]

Akhmatova's second volume of poetry, *Rosary,* was published in 1914. Many poems make allusion to places in St. Petersburg[23] and Tsarskoye Selo closely associated with her life. Others speak of love: unrequited love, a theme she had introduced in *Evening*; disappointment in love as the price paid for the poet's lyrical gifts; and passionate, earthly love juxtaposed with religious motifs. This led critic Boris Eikhenbaum to call Akhmatova "half-nun, half-harlot," a phrase that would later be picked up and used maliciously against her by the Soviet authorities. Other critics argue that these poems show her suffering to be not merely egocentric and personal but also distinctly Christian in character.

The "True Twentieth Century" Begins: 1914–1922

The outbreak of the first World War in the summer of 1914 moved Russia closer to the brink. The Germans attacked in August (19 July, Old Style), and Tsar Nicholas II assumed the role of commander-in-chief, leaving the capital in the hands of his reactionary wife Alexandra and thus, indirectly, in those of her mentor, Rasputin. The Russians suffered greater casualties than the armed forces of any other country involved in the struggle as Russian weapons were inferior, ammunition was in short supply, and vehicles often broke down. Those who remained at home endured food and fuel shortages and rampant inflation.

Akhmatova spent that summer at Slepnyovo; it was one of the last peaceful periods she would have in her life. Gumilyov enlisted immediately, hoping to prove his love for his homeland, and also to realize the role of the conquistador heroes of his own works.

In 1915, Akhmatova wrote her first great *poema* (long poem), entitled *At the Edge of the Sea (Zh. 646)*. Amanda Haight interprets it as an elegy to childhood brought to an end by contact with death.[24] The work, according to Zhirmunsky, is not a departure from her lyric poetry, but reflects "the maturation of the youthful poetic consciousness, the awakening of love and grief."[25]

Akhmatova's third collection of poetry, *White Flock,* appeared in 1917, with many of the poems written during the war. Her most famous war poems are under the general title "July 1914." In her poetry Akhmatova, like Blok, was beginning to capture the pervasive sense of doom that characterized Russia at that time.

Akhmatova's poems also reflected the growing disintegration of her marriage, as did Gumilyov's; in one of her poems, "Ah! It's you again..." *(Zh. 121),* the speaker confesses to adultery, and asks forgiveness from her stern, unyielding husband. One man that she may have been involved with was Nikolay Nedobrovo, an expressive and refined young critic recognized by many as an arbiter of artistic taste. In 1915, he published the first major article on her works, predicting her future greatness and setting her apart from sentimental female poets of the time.[26] Nedobrovo introduced Akhmatova to his friend, Boris Anrep, an artist who was posted in England during the war. He soon became a central figure in Akhmatova's life, winning her affection in a way Nedobrovo had been unable to do.[27] Anrep visited Akhmatova when he came back on brief trips to Russia, and she devoted many of her most beautiful love poems to him. He made his final departure for England in 1917. In various works written throughout her life, Akhmatova recalled the torment she felt upon his departure. She would meet him again, near the end of her life, when she stopped in Paris on her way home from receiving an honorary degree at Oxford.[28]

In 1917, power was rapidly slipping out of the Tsar's hands. In February the Tsar was deposed and a new government was born; but another authority arose at the same time — the Soviets, or councils of workers and soldiers. The competing governing bodies issued conflicting orders, compounding the chaos. In July, Alexander Kerensky became Prime Minister, but his leadership grew weaker as that of the Soviets strengthened. finally, on 25 October 1917, the Winter Palace — where the Provisional government conferred — was stormed, and the government was usurped by the Bolsheviks. The capital was moved to Moscow. Despite the fact that a peace treaty was signed with Germany in March, fighting did not end for Russia. For three years the Bolsheviks waged a bloody civil war against counter-revolutionary forces.

Akhmatova, who lived in Petersburg, had difficulties adjusting to the harshness of the post-revolutionary years, notwithstanding her anticipation of the social and political trauma that would accompany the Revolution.

In 1918, upon Gumilyov's return from Europe, Akhmatova asked for a divorce. The couple's relationship had been strained for some time and their bond was further attenuated by Gumilyov's various infidelities, which began early in the marriage and were known to Akhmatova. He was shaken by her desire to leave him and had difficulty granting her the divorce.[29]

In the same year, Akhmatova married Vladimir Shileiko, a brilliant scholar of ancient Middle Eastern texts and a poet who published in leading journals such as *Apollon* and *Hyperborean*. Shileiko worked in the research section of the Hermitage and was head of the Translators' Studio for Maxim Gorky's publishing house, All World Literature. Akhmatova knew Shileiko from the Stray Dog. Their relationship was, from the outset, challenged by harsh living conditions. For some time the couple lived in Shileiko's room in the servants' wing in Fountain House, a former palace of the noble Scheremetev family. Later, they moved to the Marble Palace on Millionnaya Street where they occupied an apartment looking out onto the field of Mars. They had two rooms which were sparsely furnished and often unheated.[30]

By 1920, Akhmatova's relationship with Shileiko had deteriorated. According to Anatoly Naiman, Akhmatova spoke about their marriage as a sad misunderstanding; nonetheless, resentment or anger often characterized the poems addressed to him.[31] Still, she continued to see Shileiko frequently, even after she left him. In 1920, Lourié helped Akhmatova get a job in the library of the Agronomy Institute, and she received an apartment on Sergievskaya Street, 7 from the Institute. In 1921, she moved in with Olga Sudeikina and Lourié who lived on the Fontanka River.[32] Akhmatova was heartbroken when he left Russia in 1922, ostensibly on a business trip to Berlin, but never to return.

Although the Civil War ended in 1921, the country was in economic turmoil. Lenin introduced the New Economic Policy (NEP), under which the state retained large industrial plants, transportation, big banks and trade, while permitting private enterprise on a small scale. Although this policy helped industry and agriculture meet the basic needs of the population, it encouraged large-scale corruption and speculation among the "NEP-men," a new breed spawned by this period.[33]

The year 1921 also brought the deaths of both Gumilyov and Blok, two major figures in the intellectual milieu as well as in Akhmatova's life. Blok died in August, exhausted and disillusioned.

In post-revolutionary Russia, Blok had been treated as an anachronism by critics, in exactly the same way as Akhmatova would be several years later.

Akhmatova learned of Gumilyov's arrest while attending Blok's funeral. He had been arrested on August 3rd for allegedly participating in a counterrevolutionary plot known as the Tagantsev Affair.[34] He was executed by a firing squad on August 25th.[35] On the eve of his arrest Gumilyov had written "Starry Horror," a poem that seemed to predict his fate: "Grief! Grief! Fear, the noose and the pit! For whomever was born on earth."[36] Akhmatova learned of his death on September 1st in a newspaper report. The funeral was on September 9th in the Kazan Cathedral. Nine years later Akhmatova would learn where he was buried and visit this communal grave for sixty people.

Another of Akhmatova's close contemporaries, Mandelstam, in contrast, survived this period. Like many of his generation, he seriously questioned the relationship between the poet and the state, a particularly trenchant issue in Russian literature with its long history of state censorship. Mandelstam believed that poetry's role was not only to educate citizens, but to address all humanity. Mandelstam's conception of the social function of Russian poetry was to influence and be reflected in Akhmatova's first post-revolutionary collection, *Plantain.* Published in 1921, *Plantain* addressed both personal and political issues.

In *Plantain,* Akhmatova dedicated several poems to Boris Anrep which suggest the range of emotions she had felt for him during the course of their relationship. While some of these poems evoke love and gratitude, others are notable for their bitterness, reproaching him for abandoning his homeland and the woman who loved him.

At the end of 1921, Akhmatova published a large collection of her works, *Anno Domini MCMXXI.* Various poems address Akhmatova's past relationships. "The Voice of Memory" *(Zh. 79),* for example, which was written on 15 September 1921, pays homage to Gumilyov, whom she remembered with grief.

Poems in the cycle "Dark Dream" refer to the effects of cold, famine, and war upon her relationship with Shileiko as the years wore on.

Poems that make allusion to the Revolution do not mention it directly but give voice to the grief and devastation that overtook the land. Akhmatova's use of "Aesopic language," which expresses what cannot be said openly by seeming to discuss another subject, is apparent.

Isolation, Terror, and War: 1922–1941

Many poets and artists failed to find a place for themselves in the new order. Akhmatova, however, remained popular among the poetry-loving public and the editions of her poems always sold out quickly.

While numerous critics responded favorably to Akhmatova's work, noting its moral consciousness and strong nationalistic character, others, including Vladimir Mayakovsky, viewed her as a relic who had not adapted to the new age. Even Kuzmin, a friend of her youth, declared that Akhmatova had lived out her role as a poet in Russian society.[37] In "Slander" *(Zh. 286),* a poignant poem written in 1922, Akhmatova depicts slander as an allegorical figure pursuing the poet. The verse was clearly written in response to attacks in the press that she viewed as malicious, opportunistic, or politically motivated. The poem was eerily prophetic of the events of 1946 when Akhmatova would be accused of having a baneful influence on the new generation, and would be expelled from the Union of Soviet Writers.

The attacks against Akhmatova were fueled in part by Leon Trotsky's dismissal of Akhmatova, among other poets, as irrelevant to the new Soviet state. These attacks culminated in 1925 when publication of her poetry was banned by an unofficial Communist Party resolution that was not made public.[38]

In 1924, Akhmatova moved with Sudeikina to another apartment on the Fontanka River; Sudeikina emigrated to Paris later that year. Beginning in 1926, Akhmatova's studies of Pushkin bore fruit in a series of insightful articles on Pushkin's life and work.

Akhmatova was seeing more of Nikolay Punin, a well known art critic and supporter of the Russian avant-garde. Haight suggests that she went to live with him in 1926. Akhmatova and Shileiko officially divorced in 1926, and he remarried. (Shileiko died of tuberculosis in October 1930.) However, she and Punin never married. They shared a small apartment in Fountain House with his former wife, Anna Arens, and their small daughter, Irina, and were joined by Akhmatova's son, Lev, in 1928.[39]

By 1928, Stalin had consolidated his position and soon launched one of the worst and most infamous periods in Soviet history: the drive to forcibly collectivize agriculture. The peasants put up an enormous resistance against losing their land by burning their crops and killing their livestock. The result was famine, which claimed victims in the millions. Purges followed, during which millions more were sent to camps or killed for alleged crimes against the state. The secret police, headed by Henryk Yagoda and later by Nikolay Yezhov, were efficient and ruthless.

The nation's greatest artists, musicians, and poets, including Osip Mandelstam, became victims of the terror. On the basis of a satirical poem he wrote against Stalin, reported by an informer, Mandelstam was arrested on 13 May 1934. Akhmatova witnessed the arrest at his Moscow apartment on Furmanov Street. He was locked up in the Lubyanka prison and though Akhmatova and Boris Pasternak appealed to influential associates of Stalin, their efforts were to no avail.

Eventually, Mandelstam and his wife were sent into exile to Voronezh, where they spent three years. Akhmatova visited them there not long before Mandelstam was arrested a second time on 1 May 1938. He died in a concentration camp in December 1938 at the age of 47.

Between 1935 and 1940, Akhmatova wrote her great cycle *Requiem,* which several friends memorized, including Lidiya Chukovskaya (1907–96), daughter of Korney Chukovsky. Often, when Akhmatova would compose a poem too dangerous to keep in written form, Chukovskaya would commit it to memory.[40]

Requiem comprises fifteen poems and was first published in 1963, in Munich. The cycle conveys the anguish of mothers whose husbands and sons are suffering, and who helplessly look on, able only to express their yearning and grief. Her own son, Lev, was first arrested in 1933, on trumped-up charges, though soon released. Both he and Punin were arrested in 1935. A letter from Akhmatova was delivered to Stalin, and they were pardoned. However, in March 1938 Lev was arrested for the third time, and this time was sentenced to 10 years in a Siberian camp. The verdict was later commuted to five years. During World War II, Lev was released to fight against the Germans.[41]

In 1937, another important person entered Akhmatova's life. Vladimir Garshin (1887–1956) was a professor, medical doctor, and member of the Academy of Medical Sciences, and a nephew of the 19th-century Russian writer, Vsevelod Garshin. He had a large collection of books on art, loved Russian poetry, and wrote verse himself. After becoming acquainted with Akhmatova when she was a patient in Leningrad's Kuibyshev Hospital, he helped her get through this very difficult period of her life. Their relationship finally led her to leave Punin; Akhmatova moved into a separate room in the Punin communal apartment.

In 1939, perhaps under the influence of his daughter Svetlana's admiration for Akhmatova's verse, Stalin allowed some of her works to be published again. Her poems appeared in journals, and in May 1940, she published a collection, *From Six Books.* In September of the same year the Central Committee of the Communist Party ordered withdrawal of the book for its allusions to religion and lack of reference to Soviet reality. However, the withdrawal came too late for the collection had sold out already.[42]

"Reed," a manuscript of poems Akhmatova worked on from 1924 to 1940, was included in *From Six Books* under the title, "Willow." (Eleven years later, she wrote a poem, also entitled "Willow," in which she returns to Tsarskoye Selo, this time in philosophical contemplation of the vagaries of fate. The willow, now only a stump, represents her friends who have long disappeared.)

Once again, war was looming. In 1940, with Hitler's shadow over Europe, Akhmatova wrote a haunting *poema* called *The Way of All the Earth (Zh. 647).* The heroine is a woman from Kitezh, a medieval city allegedly saved by prayer from a Tatar invasion. She laments for old Europe, of which only "a scrap remains." She now prays to be allowed to reach her home, to be with her people and be laid to rest.[43] Akhmatova herself would be forced to leave her home for several years, and external events would continue to impinge upon both her personal and creative life.

War with Germany was imminent. Stalin watched as Hitler seized one country after another in Eastern Europe, and on 23 August 1939 signed a pact with him, temporarily staving off the Soviet Union's participation in the global conflict. Stalin took advantage of the momentary peace to invade finland. The finns held onto their independence in this brutal war, but had to cede some territory.[44] Nonetheless, on 22 June 1941, Hitler's armies swept across the borders of the USSR. While suffering enormous losses in lives, by the close of the war the Soviet Union had made tremendous gains in territory, incorporating the Baltic states and bringing many Eastern European countries into its sphere of influence.

Along with other writers, artists, musicians and filmmakers in Leningrad and Moscow, Akhmatova was evacuated to Central Asia. She lived in the city of Tashkent in Uzbekistan until May 1944.[45] Before departing, Akhmatova addressed the women of Leningrad on the radio:

"...No, a city which has bred women like these cannot be conquered. We, the women of Leningrad, are living through difficult days, but we know that the whole of our country, all its people, are behind us. We feel their alarm for our sakes, their love and help. We thank them and we promise them that we will be ever stoic and brave."[46]

Letters and memoirs during this period chronicle Akhmatova's relationship with Garshin, who had remained in Leningrad. In October 1942, Garshin's wife collapsed on the street and died.[47]

Garshin found her in a morgue and identified her by her clothes; her face had been devoured by rats.[48] Margarita Aliger says that Garshin was haunted by this image, and it disturbed his relations with Akhmatova. Yet he continued to write to her and even proposed marriage, which she accepted.[49]

Akhmatova started home on 15 May 1944, stopping over in Moscow where she stayed with her friends, the Ardovs. Akhmatova told them and others that she was going to be married.[50] Aliger comments that she had never seen Akhmatova so happy. Her son was alive and well, her city had been liberated, and people there were waiting for her. Life would begin anew.[51]

Akhmatova's revived spirit and optimism were extinguished when Garshin met her at the railway station and informed her that they could not marry. Instead, he married a doctor[52] with whom he had worked during the war, and who had helped him survive its horrible events. Her plans suddenly derailed, Akhmatova took refuge for several months at the home of old friends, the Rybakovs.

Post-War Years: 1945–1953

In 1945, Akhmatova returned to Fountain House, where she lived with her son, who had come home after taking part in the capture of Berlin.

In April 1946, a Literary Evening was arranged at the Hall of Columns in Moscow's House of Unions, where Akhmatova and Pasternak read their works. The young people present staged an enormous ovation in honor of the two poets. This alarmed Akhmatova, who feared political repercussions.

Akhmatova, however, believed it was another incident that brought on the coming round of persecutions: the visit of the esteemed Oxford professor, Isaiah Berlin, who was in the British diplomatic corps at the time. Akhmatova's contact with the high-profile Western scholar was bound to have irritated Soviet officials, always suspicious of any relations between Soviet citizens and foreigners. She first saw him in autumn 1945 and then again on

5 January 1946 just before his return to England.[53] These meetings touched Akhmatova deeply, and she dedicated to Berlin many poems in her cycles "Sweetbrier in Blossom," "Midnight Verses," and "Cinque."

In total disregard of the patriotic poetry Akhmatova had written during the war, and despite the fact that she was a model of courage to the women of her land, the Central Committee passed a "Regulation" on 14 August 1946, condemning the magazines *Zvezda* and *Leningrad* for publishing the works of Akhmatova and those of satirical writer Mikhail Zoshchenko.[54]

Andrey Zhdanov, Secretary of the Central Committee of the Communist Party, attacked her again on 16 August 1946[55] at the Leningrad branch of the Union of Soviet Writers at the Smolny Institute, where he warned: "What positive contribution can Akhmatova's work make to our young people? It can do nothing but harm. It can only sow despondency, spiritual depression, pessimism, and the desire to walk away from the urgent questions of public life, to leave the wide paths of public life and activity for the narrow little world of personal experience. How can we place the education of young people in her hands!"[56]

Then, on 4 September 1946, Akhmatova was expelled from the Writers Union. At this time, she immersed herself again in her studies of Pushkin, working on two articles in particular, "Pushkin and Dostoevsky" and "The Death of Pushkin."

Her son, Lev, was arrested again on 6 November 1949. In 1950, Akhmatova finally decided to "repent" — to make a compromise with the Stalinist regime. She wrote "In Praise of Peace," a cycle of simple Socialist Realist verses praising the fatherland and Stalin. They were published in the magazine *Ogonyok,* but did not lead to Lev's release. Punin had been arrested shortly before on 26 August 1949; he perished in a Siberian prison camp in 1953.[57]

Last Years: 1953–1966

Stalin died on 5 March 1953. The effect of this event on Akhmatova's life was gradual but significant. She worked assiduously to free her son, who had by the late 1940s become a respected scholar of Central Asian culture, and she enlisted noted scholars to write letters on his behalf. In March 1956, Alexander Fadeyev, a high-ranking member of the Writers Union, wrote to the Chief Military Prosecutor asking for Lev's release and enclosed a letter from Akhmatova. This activity may have helped; even more significant, however, was Khrushchev's anti-Stalin speech at the 20th Party Congress that year, which led the Mikoyan Commission to speed up the return of prisoners awaiting rehabilitation. Lev was released in May and lived for a time with his mother in Leningrad. After many quarrels, he moved out, and they rarely saw each other. They always found it difficult to live together. Yet Akhmatova, as Haight points out, was extremely proud of her son and praised him highly as a scholar.[58]

In August 1956, a few months after Lev's release, Isaiah Berlin was visiting Moscow and wanted to see Akhmatova, but fearing for her son's life, she refused. She wrote about this event as a "non-meeting."

During this period, Akhmatova often stayed with friends while spending summers in Komarovo, a writer's colony outside Leningrad. She had been given a small cabin by the Literary Fund. Although she still wore her old coat and worn-out shoes, she thrived on the attention, flowers, and phone calls of admirers.[59] Four young poets were particularly attentive — Joseph Brodsky, Dmitry Bobyshev, Anatoly Naiman, and Evgeny Rein. She approved of their verse, saying they "would do," but advised them to write more concisely. Bobyshev wrote, "How happy we were. My God! Our poems were approved by Akhmatova herself, when they were rejected by every almanac, magazine, and publisher in Moscow and Leningrad. This gave us great confidence."[60]

They waited for a "dedication" — a tap of the sword on the shoulder, a symbolic "handing down of the lyre." They all devoted verses to her. Bobyshev once brought her a bouquet of five beautiful roses. Akhmatova would later say, "Four of them soon faded, but the fifth bloomed extraordinarily well and created a miracle, almost flying around the room..."[61] This inspired her to write "The fifth Rose" (Zh. 590), dedicated to Bobyshev, which she intended to become part of a three-poem "rose cycle." The others were "The Last Rose" *(S-F. I, 328–329; Zh. 480)* to Brodsky and "You — in fact..." *(Zh. 593)* to Naiman.[62]

While the four poets eventually parted, Akhmatova would bring them together once again at her funeral.

The Flight of Time, Akhmatova's least-censored collection in 40 years, appeared in 1965. It included *Reed* and her previously unpublished *Seventh Book.* One of her most famous cycles, "In the Fortieth Year" *(Zh. 347–351)*, expresses Akhmatova's horror at the bombing of London and the occupation of Paris. Another cycle, "The Wind of War" *(Zh. 352–368)*, includes poems written from July 1941 in Leningrad to 1944 in Tashkent. The most popular poem from this series, "Courage" *(Zh. 356)*, praises the power of the Russian language. The last cycle of war poems, "Victory" *(Zh. 363–367)*, written between 1942 and 1945, celebrates this "long-awaited guest."

For many years Akhmatova had been shaping *Poem Without a Hero,* the work that would crown her last years. She began it while still in Leningrad, carried on with it in Tashkent, and continued writing it into the 1960s. She writes that while going through her archives in 1940, she found letters and poems that she had not read before concerning the basis of this epic *poema,* the tragic event of 1913 in which Vsevolod Knyazev shot himself after Olga Glebova-Sudeikina rejected his passionate love for her.[63]

Due to censorship, Akhmatova employs a device that in Russian is called *tainopis,* or "secret writing," which indirectly alludes to political and personal events. In Part Two, "The Other Side of the Coin," the poet muses that she may be accused of plagiarism. The formal structure of *Poem Without a Hero,* as well as specific themes, may have been influenced by Kuzmin's long poem, *The Trout Breaks the Ice* (1929). Both poems rely on constant shifts in time and associative rather than sequential relationships of imagery. Akhmatova's poem also resembles Blok's *Retribution* — a work that looks to the past to explain present events.

The author of *Poem Without a Hero* acts like a master-of-ceremonies, introducing the protagonists and commenting on the action. As Zhirmunsky observes, "the poet is both hero and author of the poem, contemporary and guilty along with the people of her generation but at the same time a judge pronouncing a verdict over them."[64] It opens with the poet sitting in Fountain House in 1940, when guests arrive from the past. They are dressed in mummers' costumes, typical of a Russian New Year's Eve celebration of that time. In the Intermezzo, a scrap of conversation is overheard about going to the Stray Dog. The second part takes place in 1913, when the actual plot begins. A handsome young poet officer is in love with a lovely actress from the Stray Dog, but she proves unfaithful. When the young officer sees her arrive home with another lover, he commits suicide.

The poem ends with an Epilogue dated 1942, in which the poet, thousands of miles away from Leningrad, tells her beloved city now in ruins that she is inseparable from it: her shadow is on its walls, her reflection in its canals, and the sound of her footsteps is in the halls of the Hermitage Museum, the former Winter Palace of the Tsars. References are made to her "double," probably her son in exile, behind barbed wire; to death, the Noseless Slut, guarding him; and to others in the camps. Despite enormous suffering, Akhmatova remained one with her city, and with Russia. Haight summarizes what Akhmatova had discovered: "In this contrast between the world of 1913 and the 'True Twentieth Century' she finds her reward, for, despite everything, the world she lost in 1914 was incredibly poorer than the one she gained and the poet and person she was then little by comparison with what she [had] become."[65]

For many years Akhmatova had been earning her living translating works by major authors from Georgia, Serbia, Poland, India, Korea and Armenia, despite her frequent complaints that it was ruining her creativity and taking time from her own work.

In the last years of her life Akhmatova was surrounded by friends and was paid homage both at home and abroad. Robert Frost visited Russia in 1962 and went to see Akhmatova at Komarovo.[66] He was accompanied by Franklin Reeve, a young scholar and translator of Russian literature, and Mikhail Alekseyev, a Soviet specialist on Pushkin. At lunch, they asked her to recite a poem. Akhmatova chose "The Last Rose" *(S-F. I, 328–329)* written only six days before, which refers to great historical female figures who suffered for their beliefs and desires. Reeve describes the emotional effect this reading had on everyone present:

"The whole group was so caught by the immediacy of the poem and by the life and understanding which it represented that for a few seconds we were silent, still. Frost remembered this, and he also recalled Akhmatova's expression, for he commented later how grand she was but how sad she seemed to be."[67]

Although the regime became less rigid during Krushchev's era, by 1962 the political climate had again become tense, and Joseph Brodsky became a victim. Akhmatova did all she could to help him, including an appeal to Dmitry Shostakovich, who was then a member of the Supreme Soviet, but it was to no avail. He returned from exile in 1965.

In 1964, Akhmatova was awarded an Italian literary prize by the Comunita Europea Degli Scrittori (Community of European Writers), which she received in Catania, Sicily. The next year Akhmatova went to Oxford, where she received an honorary doctorate.

Afterward, she traveled through London and Paris, where she was reunited with dear friends, emigrés who had left after the Revolution. In their memoirs, many describe how moved they were to see her. Georgy Adamovich recounts the initial shock many friends had on first seeing Akhmatova again after so many years. She was no longer the slender, fashionable young Petersburg lady, but a dignified, older, portly woman whose brilliance and refined character had not changed.[68]

Akhmatova told him she believed that Russia was entering another golden age of poetry: so many young poets were now living for poetry alone, writing wonderful works. She mentioned Joseph Brodsky, calling him "a remarkable poet."[69] Adamovich describes her last moments before she left Paris, when she finally spoke about herself. "Fate did not leave anything out for me. Everything anyone could possibly experience fell to my lot."[70]

Akhmatova was never to return. After spending the summer in Komarovo, she went to Moscow in the fall and suffered a heart attack. She spent time in the hospital, stayed for awhile with the Ardovs, and then went to a convalescent home, where she died on 5 March 1966.[71] Her body was taken to a morgue in Moscow, and then flown to Leningrad. Thousands came to her funeral on March 10th at the St. Nicholas Cathedral. A ceremony also took place at the Union of Soviet Writers, where poets paid their respects by reading their poems to her. Mikhail Alekseyev spoke: "There has departed from us a poet of unheard of power, bringing fame to Russian verse far beyond the limits not only of our native city but of our entire land, because in blazing Sicily and misty Oxford they were also able to judge the power of this poetic voice."[72] She was buried in Komarovo.

В ЦАРСКОМ СЕЛЕ

1

По аллее проводят лошадок.
Длинны волны расчесанных грив.
О пленительный город загадок,
Я печальна, тебя полюбив.

Странно вспомнить: душа тосковала,
Задыхалась в предсмертном бреду.
А теперь я игрушечной стала,
Как мой розовый друг какаду.

Грудь предчувствием боли не сжата,
Если хочешь, в глаза погляди.
Не люблю только час пред закатом,
Ветер с моря и слово «уйди».

22 февраля 1911
Царское Село

IN TSARSKOYE SELO

1

They're leading the horses along the allée,
Long are the waves of combed-out manes.
Oh enchanting little town of riddles,
Though I love you, I am mournful.

It's strange to remember: my soul yearned,
It panted, delirious, near death.
Now I've become a plaything,
Like my rosy friend the cockatoo.

No hint of pain oppresses my breast,
If you like, look into my eyes.
But I don't like the hour before sunset,
The wind from the sea and the word: "Leave."

February 22, 1911
Tsarskoye Selo

2

...А там мой мраморный двойник,
Поверженный под старым кленом,
Озерным водам отдал лик,
Внимает шорохам зеленым.

И моют светлые дожди
Его запекшуюся рану...
Холодный, белый, подожди,
Я тоже мраморною стану.

1911

3

Смуглый отрок бродил по аллеям
У озерных грустил берегов,
И столетие мы лелеем
Еле слышный шелест шагов.

Иглы сосен густо и колко
Устилают низкие пни...
Здесь лежала его треуголка
И растрепанный том Парни.

24 Сентября 1911
Царское Село

2

… And there's my marble double,
Lying under the ancient maple,
He has given his face to the waters of the lake,
And he's listening to the green rustling.

And bright rainwater washes
His clotted wound …
Cold one, white one, wait,
I'll become marble too.

1911

3

A dark-skinned youth wandered along these allées,
By the shores of this lake he yearned,
And a hundred years later we cherish
The rustle of steps, faintly heard.

A layer of pine needles covers
The stumps with a thick, bristly mat …
Here lay his tattered copy of Parny
And his three-cornered hat.

September 24, 1911
Tsarskoe Selo

Сжала руки под темной вуалью...
«Отчего ты сегодня бледна?»
— Оттого, что я терпкой печалью
Напоила его допьяна.

Как забуду? Он вышел, шатаясь,
Искривился мучительно рот...
Я сбежала, перил не касаясь,
Я бежала за ним до ворот.

Задыхаясь, я крикнула: «Шутка
Все, что было. Уйдешь, я умру».
Улыбнулся спокойно и жутко
И сказал мне: «Не стой на ветру».

8 января 1911
Киев

Under her dark veil she wrung her hands …
"Why are you so pale today?"
"Because I made him drink of stinging grief
Until he got drunk on it.

How can I forget? He staggered out,
His mouth twisted in agony …
I ran down not touching the banister
And caught up with him at the gate.

Panting, I cried: 'A joke!
That's all it was. If you leave, I'll die.'
He smiled calmly and grimly
And told me: 'Don't stand here in the wind.'"

January 8, 1911
Kiev

Память о солнце в сердце слабеет.
Желтей трава.
Ветер снежинками ранними веет
Едва-едва.

В узких каналах уже не струится —
Стынет вода.
Здесь никогда ничего не случится, —
О, никогда!

Ива на небе пустом распластала
Веер сквозной.
Может быть лучше, что я не стала
Вашей женой.

Память о солнце в сердце слабеет.
Что это? Тьма?
Может быть!.. За ночь прийти успеет
Зима.

30 января 1911
Киев

The heart's memory of the sun grows faint.
The grass is yellower.
A few early snowflakes blow in the wind,
Barely, barely.

The narrow canals have stopped flowing —
The water is chilling.
Nothing will ever happen here —
Oh, never!

The willow spreads its transparent fan
Against the empty sky.
Perhaps I should not have become
Your wife.

The heart's memory of the sun grows faint.
What's this? Darkness?
It could be! … One night brings winter's first
Hard freeze.

January 30, 1911
Kiev

ПЕСНЯ ПОСЛЕДНЕЙ ВСТРЕЧИ

Так беспомощно грудь холодела,
Но шаги мои были легки.
Я на правую руку надела
Перчатку с левой руки.

Показалось, что много ступеней,
А я знала – их только три!
Между кленов шепот осенний
Попросил: «Со мною умри!

Я обманут моей унылой,
Переменчивой, злой судьбой».
Я ответила: «Милый, милый!
И я тоже умру с тобой...»

Это песня последней встречи.
Я взглянула на темный дом.
Толко в спальне горели свечи
Равнодушно-желтым огнем.

29 сентября 1911
Царское село

THE SONG OF THE LAST MEETING

Then helplessly my breast grew cold,
But my steps were light.
I pulled the glove for my left hand
Onto my right.

There seemed to be many steps,
But I knew — there were only three!
The whisper of autumn in the maples
Was pleading: "Die with me!"

I am betrayed by my doleful,
Fickle, evil fate."
I answered: "Darling, darling!
I too. I will die with you …"

This is the song of the last meeting.
I glanced at the dark house.
Candles were burning only in the bedroom,
With an indifferent-yellow flame.

September 29, 1911
Tsarskoye Selo

Мне с тобою пьяным весело —
Смысла нет в твоих рассказах.
Осень ранняя развесила
Флаги желтые на вязах.

Оба мы в страну обманную
Забрели и горько каемся,
Но зачем улыбкой странною
И застывшей улыбаемся?

Мы хотели муки жалящей
Вместо счастья безмятежного...
Не покину я товарища
И беспутного и нежного.

1911
Париж

When you're drunk it's so much fun —
Your stories don't make sense.
An early fall has strung
The elms with yellow flags.

We've strayed into the land of deceit
And we're repenting bitterly,
Why then are we smiling these
Strange and frozen smiles?

We wanted piercing anguish
Instead of placid happiness …
I won't abandon my comrade,
So dissolute and mild.

1911
Paris

СЕРОГЛАЗЫЙ КОРОЛЬ

Слава тебе, безысходная боль!
Умер вчера сероглазый король.

Вечер осенний был душен и ал,
Муж мой, вернувшись, спокойно сказал:

«Знаешь, с охоты его принесли,
Тело у старого дуба нашли.

Жаль королеву. Такой молодой!..
За ночь одну она стала седой».

Трубку свою на камине нашел
И на работу ночную ушел.

Дочку мою я сейчас разбужу,
В серые глазки ее погляжу.

А за окном шелестят тополя:
«Нет на земле твоего короля...»

11 декабря 1910
Царское Село

THE GRAY-EYED KING

Hail to thee, everlasting pain!
The gray-eyed king died yesterday.

Scarlet and close was the autumn eve,
My husband, returning, said calmly to me:

"They brought him back from the hunt, you know,
They found his body near the old oak.

Pity the queen. So young! . .
Overnight her hair has turned gray."

Then he found his pipe on the hearth
And left, as he did every night, for work.

I will wake my little daughter now,
And look into her eyes of gray.

And outside the window the poplars whisper:
"Your king is no more on this earth ..."

December 11, 1910
Tsarskoye Selo

Он любил...

Он любил три вещи на свете:
За вечерней пенье, белых павлинов
И стертые карты Америки.
Не любил, когда плачут дети,
Не любил чая с малиной
И женской истерики.
...А я была его женой.

9 ноябрь 1910
Киев

He loved …

He loved three things in life:
Evensong, white peacocks
And old maps of America.
He hated it when children cried,
He hated tea with raspberry jam
And women's hysterics.
… And I was his wife.

November 9, 1910
Kiev

Вере Ивановой-Шварсалон

Туманом легким парк наполнился,
И вспыхнул на воротах газ.
Мне только взгляд один запомнился
Незнающих, спокойных глаз.

Твоя печаль, для всех неявная,
Мне сразу сделалась близка,
И поняла ты, что отравная
И душная во мне тоска.

Я этот день люблю и праздную,
Приду, как только позовешь.
Меня, и грешную, и праздную,
Лишь ты одна не упрекнешь.

Апрель 1911

— to Vera Ivanova-Shvarsalon

The park was filled with light mist,
And the gaslight flared at the gate.
I remember only a certain gaze
From ingenuous, tranquil eyes.

Your sorrow, unperceived by all the rest,
Immediately drew me close,
And you understood that yearning
Was poisoning and stifling me.

I love this day and I'm celebrating,
I will come as soon as you invite me.
And sinful and idle, I know
That you alone will not indict me.

April 1911

И когда друг друга проклинали
В страсти раскаленной добела,
Оба мы еще не понимали,
Как земля для двух людей мала,
И что память яростная мучит,
Пытка сильных — огненный недуг! —
И в ночи бездонной сердце учит
Спрашивать: о, где ушедший друг?
А когда, сквозь волны фимиама,
Хор гремит, ликуя и грозя,
Смотрят в душу строго и упрямо
Те же неизбежные глаза.

1909

And when we had cursed each other,
Passionate, white hot,
We still didn't understand
How small the earth can be for two people,
And that memory can torment savagely.
The anguish of the strong — a wasting disease!
And in the endless night the heart learns
To ask: Oh, where is my departed lover?
And when, through waves of incense,
The choir thunders, exulting and threatening,
Those same eyes, inescapable,
Stare sternly and stubbornly into the soul.

1909

Меня покинул в новолунье
Мой друг любимый. Ну так что ж!
Шутил: «Канатная плясунья!
Как ты до мая доживешь?»

Ему ответила, как брату,
Я, не ревнуя, не ропща,
Но не заменят мне утрату
Четыре новые плаща.

Пусть страшен путь мой, пусть опасен.
Еще страшнее путь тоски...
Как мой китайский зонтик красен,
Натерты мелом башмачки!

Оркестр веселое играет,
И улыбаются уста.
Но сердце знает, сердце знает,
Что ложа пятая пуста!

Ноябрь 1911
Царское Село

At the new moon he abandoned me,
My beloved friend. Well, so what?
"Rope dancer!" he mocked,
"How will you live until May?"

I answered him as if he were a brother,
Without grumbling, without jealousy,
But four new cloaks
Haven't made up the loss to me.

Frightening and dangerous is the path I walk,
But the path of yearning is more terrible …
How red, my Chinese parasol,
And the soles of my slippers are chalked!

The orchestra strikes up something gay
And my lips smile.
But my heart knows, my heart knows,
The fifth loge is empty!

November 1911
Tsarskoye Selo

ПРОГУЛКА

Перо задело о верх экипажа,
Я поглядела в глаза его.
Томилось сердце, не зная даже
Причины горя своего.

Безветрен вечер и грустью скован
Под сводом облачных небес,
И словно тушью нарисован
В альбоме старом Булонский лес.

Бензина запах и сирени,
Насторожившийся покой...
Он снова тронул мои колени
Почти не дрогнувшей рукой.

Май 1913

OUTING

My feather brushed the top of the carriage.
I glanced into his eyes.
My heart ached, not really
Knowing why.

The evening was windless and fettered by sadness
Under the firmament's vault of clouds,
And the Bois de Boulogne looked as if it were drawn
In India ink in some old album.

There's an odor of petrol and lilacs,
Quiet listens expectantly ...
With a hand almost not trembling
Once again he touched my knees.

May 1913

Все мы бражники здесь, блудницы,
Как невесело вместе нам!
На стенах цветы и птицы
Томятся по облакам.

Ты куришь черную трубку,
Так странен дымок над ней.
Я надела узкую юбку,
Чтоб казаться еще стройней.

Навсегда забиты окошки.
Что там — изморозь или гроза?
На глаза осторожной кошки
Похожи твои глаза.

О, как сердце мое тоскует!
Не смертного ль часа жду?
А та, что сейчас танцует,
Непременно будет в аду.

1 января 1913

We are all carousers and loose women here;
How unhappy we are together!
The flowers and birds on the wall
Yearn for the clouds.

You are smoking a black pipe,
The puff of smoke has a funny shape.
I've put on my tight skirt
To make myself look still more svelte.

The windows are sealed tight.
What's out there — hoarfrost or a storm?
You gaze with the eyes
Of a cautious cat.

Oh, I am sick at heart!
Isn't it the hour of death I await?
But that woman dancing now
Will be in hell, no doubt.

January 1, 1913

Столько просьб у любимой всегда!
У разлюбленной просьб не бывает.
Как я рада, что нынче вода
Под бесцветным ледком замирает.

И я стану — Христос помоги! —
На покров этот, светлый и ломкий,
А ты письма мои береги.
Чтобы нас рассудили потомки,

Чтоб отчетливей и ясней
Ты был виден им, мудрый и смелый.
В биографии славной твоей
Разве можно оставить пробелы?

Слишком сладко земное питье,
Слишком плотны любовные сети.
Пусть когда-нибудь имя мое
Прочитают в учебнике дети,

И, печальную повесть узнав,
Пусть они улыбнутся лукаво...
Мне любви и покоя не дав,
Подари меня горькою славой.

1913

How many demands the beloved can make!
The woman discarded, none.
How glad I am that today the water
Under the colorless ice is motionless.

And I stand — Christ help me! —
On this shroud that is brittle and bright,
But save my letters
So that our descendants can decide,

So that you, courageous and wise,
Will be seen by them with greater clarity.
Perhaps we may leave some gaps
In your glorious biography?

Too sweet is earthly drink,
Too tight the nets of love.
Sometime let the children read
My name in their lesson book,

And on learning the sad story,
Let them smile slyly …
Since you've given me neither love nor peace,
Grant me bitter glory.

1913

В последний раз мы встретились тогда
На набережной, где всегда встречались.
Была в Неве высокая вода,
И наводненья в городе боялись.

Он говорил о лете и о том,
Что быть поэтом женщине — нелепость.
Как я запомнила высокий царский дом
И Петропавловскую крепость! —

Затем, что воздух был совсем не наш,
А как подарок Божий — так чудесен.
И в этот час была мне отдана
Последняя из всех безумных песен.

Январь 1914

We met for the last time
On the embankment, where we had always met.
The Neva was high
And they were afraid the city would flood.

He spoke of the summer, and he also said
That for a woman to be a poet was — absurd.
I can still see the tsar's tall palace
And the Peter and Paul fortress! —

Because the air was not ours at all,
But like a gift from God — so miraculous.
And at that moment was given to me
The latest of all my mad songs.

January 1914

М. Лозинскому

Он длится без конца — янтарный, тяжкий день!
Как невозможна грусть, как тщетно ожиданье!
И снова голосом серебряным олень
В зверинце говорит о северном сиянье.
И я поверила, что есть прохладный снег
И синяя купель для тех, кто нищ и болен,
И санок маленьких такой неверный бег
Под звоны древние далеких колоколен.

1913

— to M. Lozinsky

It drags on forever — this heavy, amber day!
How unsufferable is grief, how futile the wait!
And once more comes the silver voice of the deer
From the menagerie, telling of the northern lights.
And I, too, believed that somewhere there was cold snow,
And a bright blue font for the poor and the ill,
And the unsteady dash of little sleighs
Under the ancient droning of distant bells.

1913

Я научилась просто, мудро жить,
Смотреть на небо и молиться Богу,
И долго перед вечером бродить,
Чтоб утомить ненужную тревогу.

Когда шурщат в овраге лопухи
И никнет гроздь рябины желто-красной,
Слагаю я веселые стихи
О жизни тленной, тленной и прекрасной.

Я возвращаюсь. Лижет мне ладонь
Пушистый кот, мурлыкает умильней,
И яркий загорается огонь
На башенке озерной лесопильни.

Лишь изредка прорезывает тишь
Крик аиста, слетевшего на крышу.
И если в дверь мою ты постучишь,
Мне кажется, я даже не услышу.

1912

I've learned to live simply, wisely,
To look at the sky and pray to God,
And to take long walks before evening
To wear out this useless anxiety.

When the burdocks rustle in the ravine
And the yellow-red clusters of rowan nod,
I compose happy verses
About mortal life, mortal and beautiful life.

I return. The fluffy cat
Licks my palm and sweetly purrs.
And on the turret of the sawmill by the lake
A bright flame flares.

The quiet is cut, occasionally,
By the cry of a stork landing on the roof.
And if you were to knock at my door,
It seems to me I wouldn't even hear.

1912

ИСПОВЕДЬ

Умолк простивший мне грехи.
Лиловый сумрак гасит свечи.
И темная епитрахиль
Накрыла голову и плечи.

Не тот ли голос: «Дева! встань...»
Удары сердца чаще, чаще.
Прикосновение сквозь ткань
Руки, рассеянно крестящей.

1911
Царское Село

CONFESSION

Having forgiven me my sins, he fell silent.
In the violet dusk candles sputtered,
And a dark prayer stole
Covered my head and my shoulders.

Isn't that the voice that said: "Maiden! Arise ..."
My heart beats faster, faster.
The touch, through the cloth,
Of a hand absently making the sign of the cross.

1911
Tsarskoye Selo

Протертый коврик под иконой,
В прохладной комнате темно,
И густо плющ темно-зеленый
Завил широкое окно.

От роз струится запах сладкий,
Трещит лампадка, чуть горя.
Пестро расписаны укладки
Рукой любовной кустаря.

И у окна белеют пяльцы...
Твой профиль тонок и жесток.
Ты зацелованные пальцы
Брезгливо прячешь под платок.

А сердцу стало страшно биться,
Такая в нем теперь тоска...
И в косах спутанных таится
Чуть слышный запах табака.

1912

Under the icon, a threadbare rug,
It's dark in the chilly room,
And dark green ivy thickly
Twines around the wide window.

A sweet scent streams from the roses,
The icon lamp sputters, barely aglow.
There are chests, floridly painted
By the craftsman's loving hand.

And near the window a white lace frame …
Your profile is sharp and drawn.
And under your handkerchief you conceal with disgust
fingers that have just been kissed.

And the heart that began to pound,
How much anguish it holds now …
And in the disheveled braids lurks
The smell of tobacco smoke.

1912

ГОСТЬ

Всё как раньше: в окна столовой
Бьется мелкий метельный снег,
И сама я не стала новой,
А ко мне приходил человек.

Я спросила: “Чего ты хочешь?”
Он сказал: “Быть с тобой в аду”.
Я смеялась: “Ах, напророчишь
Нам обоим, пожалуй, беду”.

Но, поднявши руку сухую,
Он слегка потрогал цветы:
“Расскажи, как тебя целуют,
Расскажи, как целуешь ты”.

И глаза, глядевшие тускло,
Не сводил с моего кольца.
Ни один не двинулся мускул
Просветленно-злого лица.

О, я знаю: его отрада —
Напряженно и страстно знать,
Что ему ничего не надо,
Что мне не в чем ему отказать.

1 января 1914

THE GUEST

Everything is the same: a fine snowstorm
Beats against the windows of the dining room,
And even I haven't changed,
But a man approached me.

I asked: "What do you want?"
He said: "To be with you in hell."
I laughed: "Ah, then you prophesy,
For both of us, calamity."

But raising his dry hand,
He lightly brushed the flowers:
"Tell me how they kiss you,
Tell me how you kiss."

And he stared at my ring
With fixed, lackluster eyes.
Not a single muscle moved
On his radiant, evil face.

Oh, I know: his consolation —
To realize with passionate intensity
That he needs nothing,
That I have nothing to refuse him.

January 1, 1914

УЕДИНЕНИЕ

Так много камней брошено в меня,
Что ни один из них уже не страшен,
И стройной башней стала западня,
Высокою среди высоких башен.
Строителей ее благодарю,
Пусть их забота и печаль минует.
Отсюда раньше вижу я зарю,
Здесь солнца луч последний торжествует.
И часто в окна комнаты моей
Влетают ветры северных морей,
И голубь ест из рук моих пшеницу...
А не дописанную мной страницу,
Божественно спокойна и легка,
Допишет Музы смуглая рука.

6 июня 1914
Слепнево

SOLITUDE

So many stones have been thrown at me,
That I'm not frightened of them any more,
And the pit has become a solid tower,
Tall among tall towers.
I thank the builders,
May care and sadness pass them by.
From here I'll see the sunrise earlier,
Here the sun's last ray rejoices.
And into the windows of my room
The northern breezes often fly.
And from my hand a dove eats grains of wheat …
As for my unfinished page,
The Muse's tawny hand, divinely calm
And delicate, will finish it.

June 6, 1914
Slepnyovo

М. Лозинскому

Они летят, они еще в дороге,
Слова освобожденья и любви,
А я уже в предпесенной тревоге,
И холоднее льда уста мои.

Но скоро там, где жидкие березы,
Прильнувши к окнам, сухо шелестят, —
Венцом червонным заплетутся розы,
И голоса незримых прозвучат.

А дальше — свет невыносимо щедрый,
Как красное горячее вино...
Уже душистым, раскаленным ветром
Сознание мое опалено.

Лето 1916
Слепнево

— to M. Lozinsky

They are flying, they are still on their way,
The words of love and release.
I feel that uneasiness that comes before a poem,
And my lips are cold as ice.

But there, where a few scraggly birches
Cling to the windows and rustle dryly —
A dark red wreath of roses twines
And the voices of invisible speakers resound.

And farther on — a light unbearably lavish,
Like hot red wine …
Already a fragrant, burning wind
Sears my consciousness.

Summer 1916
Slepnyovo

Н.В.Н

Есть в близости людей заветная черта,
Ее не перейти влюбленности и страсти, —
Пусть в жуткой тишине сливаются уста
И сердце рвется от любви на части.

И дружба здесь бессильна и года
Высокого и огненного счастья,
Когда душа свободна и чужда
Медлительной истоме сладострастья.

Стремящиеся к ней безумны, а ее
Достигшие — поражены тоскою...
Теперь ты понял, отчего мое
Не бьется сердце под твоей рукою.

Май 1915
Петербург

N. V. N.

There is a sacred boundary between those who are close
And it cannot be crossed by passion or love —
Though lips fuse in dreadful silence
And the heart shatters to pieces with love.

Friendship is helpless here, and years
Of exalted and ardent happiness,
When the soul is free and a stranger
To the slow languor of voluptuousness.

Those who strive to reach it are mad, and those
Who reach it — stricken by grief …
Now you understand why my heart
Does not beat faster under your hand.

May 1915
Petersburg

Нам свежесть слов и чувства простоту
Терять не то ль, что живописцу — зренье,
Или актеру — голос и движенье,
А женщине прекрасной — красоту?

Но не пытайся для себя хранить
Тебе дарованное небесами:
Осуждены — и это знаем сами —
Мы расточать, а не копить.

Иди один и исцеляй слепых,
Чтобы узнать в тяжелый час сомненья
Учеников злорадное глумленье
И равнодушие толпы.

23 июня 1915
Слепнево

For us to lose freshness of words and simplicity of feeling,
Isn't it the same as for a painter to lose — sight,
Or an actor — his voice and movement,
Or a beautiful woman — beauty?

But don't try to save for yourself
This heaven-sent gift:
We are condemned — and we know this ourselves —
To squander it, not hoard it.

Walk alone and heal the blind,
In order to know in the heavy hour of doubt
The gloating mockery of disciples,
And the indifference of the crowd.

June 23, 1915
Slepnyovo

Ведь где-то есть простая жизнь и свет,
Прозрачный, теплый и веселый...
Там с девушкой через забор сосед
Под вечер говорит, и слышат только пчелы
Нежнейшую из всех бесед.

А мы живем торжественно и трудно
И чтим обряды наших горьких встреч,
Когда с налету ветер безрассудный
Чуть начатую обрывает речь, —

Но ни на что не променяем пышный
Гранитный город славы и беды,
Широких рек сияющие льды,
Бессолнечные, мрачные сады
И голос Музы еле слышный.

23 июня 1915
Слепнево

Somewhere there is a simple life and a world,
Transparent, warm, joyful …
There at evening a neighbor talks with a girl
Across the fence, and only the bees can hear
This most tender murmuring of all.

But we live ceremoniously and with difficulty
And we observe the rites of our bitter meetings,
When suddenly the reckless wind
Breaks off a sentence just begun —

But not for anything would we exchange this splendid
Granite city of fame and calamity,
The wide rivers of glistening ice,
The sunless, gloomy gardens,
And, barely audible, the muse's voice.

June 23, 1915
Slepnyovo

ИЮЛЬ 1914

1

Пахнет гарью. Четыре недели
Торф сухой по болотам горит,
Даже птицы сегодня не пели
И осина уже не дрожит.

Стало солнце немилостью божьей,
Дождик с Пасхи долей не кропил.
Приходил одноногий прохожий
И один на дворе говорил:

«Сроки страшные близятся. Скоро
Станет тесно от свежих могил.
Ждите глада, и труса, и мора,
И затменья небесных светил.

Только нашей земли не разделит
На потеху себе супостат:
Богородица белый расстелет
Над скорбями великими плат».

JULY 1914

1

It smells of burning. For four weeks
The dry peat bog has been burning.
The birds have not even sung today ,
And the aspen has stopped quaking.

The sun has become God's displeasure,
Rain has not sprinkled the fields since Easter.
A one-legged stranger came along
And all alone in the courtyard he said:

"Fearful times are drawing near. Soon
Fresh graves will be everywhere.
There will be famine, earthquakes, widespread death,
And the eclipse of the sun and the moon.

But the enemy will not divide
Our land at will, for himself:
The Mother of God will spread her white mantle
Over this enormous grief."

2

Можжевельника запах сладкий
От горящих лесов летит.
Над ребятами стонут солдатки,
Вдовий плач по деревне звенит.

Не напрасно молебны служились,
О дожде тосковала земля!
Красной влагой тепло окропились
Затоптанные поля.

Низко, низко небо пустое,
И голос молящего тих:
«Ранят тело твое пресвятое,
Мечут жребий о ризах твоих»

20 июля 1914
Слепчево

2

The sweet smell of juniper
flies from the burning woods.
Soldiers' wives are wailing for the boys,
The widow's lament keens over the countryside.

The public prayers were not in vain,
The earth was yearning for rain!
Warm red liquid sprinkled
The trampled fields.

Low, low hangs the empty sky
And a praying voice quietly intones:
"They are wounding your sacred body,
They are casting lots for your robes."

July 20, 1914
Slepnyovo

ПАМЯТИ 19 ИЮЛЯ 1914

Мы на сто лет состарились, и это
Тогда случилось в час один:
Короткое уже кончалось лето,
Дымилось тело вспаханных равнин;

Вдруг запестрела тихая дорога,
Плач полетел, серебряно звеня.
Закрыв лицо, я умоляла Бога
До первой битвы умертвить меня.

Из памяти, как груз отныне лишний,
Исчезли тени песен и страстей,
Ей — опустевшей — приказал Всевышний
Стать страшной книгой грозовых вестей.

Лето 1916
Слепнево

IN MEMORIAM, JULY 19, 1914

We aged a hundred years, and this
Happened in a single hour:
The short summer had already died,
The body of the ploughed plains smoked.

Suddenly the quiet road burst into color,
A lament flew up, ringing, silver …
Covering my face, I implored God
Before the first battle to strike me dead.

Like a burden henceforth unnecessary,
The shadows of passion and songs vanished from my memory.
The Most High ordered it — emptied —
To become a grim book of calamity.

Summer 1916
Slepnyovo

Я не знаю, ты жив или умер, —
На земле тебя можно искать
Или только в вечерней думе
По усопшем светло горевать.

Всё тебе: и молитва дневная,
И бессонницы млеющий жар,
И стихов моих белая стая,
И очей моих синий пожар.

Мне никто сокровенней не был,
Так меня никто не томил,
Даже тот, кто на муку предал,
Даже тот, кто ласкал и забыл.

Лето 1915
Слепнево

I don't know if you're living or dead —
Whether to look for you here on earth
Or only in evening meditation,
When we grieve serenely for the dead.

Everything is for you: my daily prayer,
And the thrilling fever of the insomniac,
And the blue fire of my eyes,
And my poems, that white flock.

No one was more intimate with me,
No one made me suffer so,
Not even the one who consigned me to torment,
Not even the one who caressed and forgot.

Summer 1915
Slepnyovo

Двадцать первое. Ночь. Понедельник.
Очертанья столицы во мгле.
Сочинил же какой-то бездельник,
Что бывает любовь на земле.

И от лености или со скуки
Все поверили, так и живут:
Ждут свиданий, боятся разлуки
И любовные песни поют.

Но иным открывается тайна,
И почиет на них тишина...
Я на это наткнулась случайно
И с тех пор все как будто больна.

1917
Петербург

The twenty-first. Night. Monday.
The outlines of the capital are in mist.
Some idler invented the idea
That there's something in the world called love.

And from laziness or boredom,
Everyone believed it and here is how they live:
They anticipate meetings, they fear partings
And they sing the songs of love.

But the secret will be revealed to the others,
And a hush will fall on them all …
I stumbled on it by accident
And since then have been somehow unwell.

1917
Petersburg

Стал мне реже сниться, слава Богу,
Больше не мерещится везде.
Лег туман на белую дорогу,
Тени побежали по воде.

И весь день не замолкали звоны
Над простором вспаханной земли,
Здесь всего сильнее от Ионы
Колокольни Лаврские вдали.

Подстригаю на кустах сирени
Ветки те, что нынче отцвели;
По валам старинных укреплений
Два монаха медленно прошли.

Мир родной, понятный и телесный
Для меня незрячей оживи.
Исцелил мне душу Царь Небесный
Ледяным покоем нелюбви.

1912
Киев

I dream of him less often now, thank God,
He doesn't appear everywhere anymore.
Fog lies on the white road,
Shadows start to run along the water.

And the ringing goes on all day.
Over the endless expanse of ploughed fields,
Ever louder sound the bells
From Jonah's Monastery far away.

I am clipping today's wilted branches
From the lilac bushes;
On the ramparts of the ancient fortress,
Two monks stroll.

Revive for me, who cannot see,
The familiar, comprehensible, corporeal world.
The heavenly king has already healed my soul
With the peace of unlove, icy cold.

1912
Kiev

Как люблю, как любила глядеть я
На закованные берега,
На балконы, куда столетья
Не ступала ничья нога.
И воистину ты, столица —
Для безумных и светлых нас;
Но когда над Невою длится
Тот особенный, чистый час
И проносится ветер майский
Мимо всех надводных колонн,
Ты — как грешник, видящий райский
Перед смертью сладчайший сон...

1916

How I love, how I loved to look
At your chained shores,
At the balconies, where for hundreds of years
No one has set foot.
And verily you are the capital
For us who are mad and luminous;
But when that special, pure hour
Lingers over the Neva
And the May wind sweeps
Past all the columns lining the water,
You are like a sinner turning his eyes,
Before death, to the sweetest dream of paradise …

1916

Я слышу иволги всегда печальный голос
И лета пышного приветствую ущерб,
А к колосу прижатый тесно колос
С змеиным свистом срезывает серп.

И стройных жниц короткие подолы,
Как флаги в праздник, по ветру летят.
Теперь бы звон бубенчиков веселых,
Сквозь пыльные ресницы долгий взгляд.

Не ласки жду я, не любовной лести
В предчувствии неотвратимой тьмы,
Но приходи взглянуть на рай, где вместе
Блаженны и невинны были мы.

27 июля 1917
Слепнево

I am listening to the orioles' ever mournful voice
And saluting the splendid summer's decline.
And through grain pressed tightly, ear to ear,
The sickle, with its snake's hiss, slices.

And the short skirts of the slender reapers
fly in the wind, like flags on a holiday.
The jingling of bells would be jolly now,
And through dusty lashes, a long, slow gaze.

It's not caresses I await, nor lover's adulation,
The premonition of inevitable darkness,
But come with me to gaze at paradise, where together
We were innocent and blessed.

July 27, 1917
Slepnyovo

Теперь никто не станет слушать песен.
Предсказанные наступили дни.
Моя последняя, мир больше не чудесен,
Не разрывай мне сердца, не звени.

Еще недавно ласточкой свободной
Свершала ты свой утренний полет,
А ныне станешь нищенкой голодной,
Не достучишься у чужих ворот.

1917

Now no one will listen to songs.
The prophesied days have begun.
Latest poem of mine, the world has lost its wonder,
Don't break my heart, don't ring out.

A while ago, free as a swallow,
You accomplished your morning flight,
But now you've become a hungry beggar,
Knocking in vain at strangers' gates.

1917

По твердому гребню сугроба
В твой белый, таинственный дом
Такие притихшие оба
В молчании нежном идем.
И слаще всех песен пропетых
Мне этот исполненный сон,
Качание веток задетых
И шпор твоих легонький звон.

Январь 1917

Over the snowdrift's hard crust
Into your white, mysterious house,
We walk in tender silence,
Both hushed.
And sweeter to me than all songs sung
Is this dream fulfilled,
The gentle clinking of your spurs
And the swaying of branches we've brushed.

January 1917

Когда в тоске самоубийства
Народ гостей немецких ждал,
И дух суровый византийства
От русской Церкви отлетал;
Когда приневская столица,
Забыв величие своё,
Как опьяневшая блудница,
Не знала, кто берёт ее,
Мне голос был. Он звал утешно,
Он говорил: "Иди сюда,
Оставь свой край, глухой и грешный,
Оставь Россию навсегда.
Я кровь от рук твоих отмою,
Из сердца выну черный стыд,
Я новым именем покрою
Боль поражений и обид".
Но равнодушно и спокойно
Руками я замкнула слух,
Чтоб этой речью недостойной
Не осквернился скорбный дух.

Осень 1917

And when in suicidal anguish
The nation awaited its German guests,
And the stern spirit of Byzantium
Had fled from the Russian Church,
When the capital by the Neva,
Forgetting her greatness,
Like a drunken prostitute
Did not know who would take her next,
A voice came to me. It called out comfortingly,
It said, "Come here,
Leave your deaf and sinful land,
Leave Russia forever.
I will wash the blood from your hands,
Root out the black shame from your heart,
With a new name I will conceal
The pain of defeats and injuries."
But calmly and indifferently,
I covered my ears with my hands,
So that my sorrowing spirit
Would not be stained by those shameful words.

Autumn 1917

ПЕТРОГРАД, 1919

И мы забыли навсегда,
Заключены в столице дикой,
Озера, степи, города
И зори родины великой.
В кругу кровавом день и ночь
Долит жестокая истома...
Никто нам не хотел помочь
За то, что мы остались дома,
За то, что, город свой любя,
А не крылатую свободу,
Мы сохранили для себя
Его дворцы, огонь и воду.

Иная близится пора,
Уж ветер смерти сердце студит,
Но нам священный град Петра
Невольным памятником будет.

PETROGRAD, 1919

And confined to this savage capital,
We have forgotten forever
The lakes, the steppes, the towns,
And the dawns of our great native land.
Day and night in the bloody circle
A brutal languor overcomes us …
No one wants to help us
Because we stayed home,
Because, loving our city
And not winged freedom,
We preserved for ourselves
Its palaces, its fire and water.

A different time is drawing near,
The wind of death already chills the heart,
But the holy city of Peter
Will be our unintended monument.

Не с теми я, кто бросил землю
На растерзание врагам.
Их грубой лести я не внемлю,
Им песен я своих не дам.

Но вечно жалок мне изгнанник,
Как заключенный, как больной.
Темна твоя дорога, странник,
Полынью пахнет хлеб чужой.

А здесь, в глухом чаду пожара
Остаток юности губя,
Мы ни единого удара
Не отклонили от себя.

И знаем, что в оценке поздней
Оправдан будет каждый час...
Но в мире нет людей бесслезней,
Надменнее и проще нас.

Июль 1922
Петербург

I am not with those who abandoned their land
To the lacerations of the enemy.
I am deaf to their coarse flattery,
I won't give them my songs.

But to me the exile is forever pitiful,
Like a prisoner, like someone ill.
Dark is your road, wanderer,
Like wormwood smells the bread of strangers.

But here, in the blinding smoke of the conflagration
Destroying what's left of youth,
We have not deflected from ourselves
One single stroke.

And we know that in the final accounting,
Each hour will be justified …
But there is no people on earth more tearless
More simple and more full of pride.

July 1922
Petersburg

Тебе покорной? Ты сошел с ума!
Покорна я одной Господней воле.
Я не хочу ни трепета, ни боли,
Мне муж — палач, а дом его — тюрьма.

Но видишь ли! Ведь я пришла сама...
Декабрь рождался, ветры выли в поле,
И было так светло в твоей неволе,
А за окошком сторожила тьма.

Так птица о прозрачное стекло
Всем телом бьется в зимнее ненастье,
И кровь пятнает белое крыло.

Теперь во мне спокойствие и счастье.
Прощай, мой тихий, ты мне вечно мил
За то, что в дом свой странницу пустил.

Август 1921

Submissive to you? You're out of your mind!
I submit only to the will of the Lord.
I want neither thrills nor pain,
My husband — is a hangman, and his home — prison.

Well, look here! I came of my own accord ...
It was already December, the winds were abroad,
And it was so bright in your bondage,
But outside the window, darkness stood guard.

Thus in the wintry blast, a bird
Beats its whole body against the clear glass,
And blood stains its white wing.

Now I have peace and good fortune.
Goodbye, you are dear to me forever, gentle one,
Because you let this pilgrim into your home.

August 1921

Шепчет: «Я не пожалею
Даже то, что так люблю, —
Или будь совсем моею,
Или я тебя убью».
Надо мной жужжит, как овод,
Непрестанно столько дней
Этот самый скучный довод
Черной ревности твоей.
Горе душит — не задушит,
Вольный ветер слезы сушит,
А веселье, чуть погладит,
Сразу с бедным сердцем сладит.

Февраль 1922

He whispers, "I'm not sorry
For loving you this way —
Either be mine alone
Or I will kill you."
It buzzes around me like a gadfly,
Incessantly, day after day,
This same boring argument,
Your black jealousy.
Grief smothers — but not fatally,
The wide wind dries my tears
And cheerfulness begins to soothe,
To smooth out this troubled heart.

February 1922

ЛОТОВА ЖЕНА

Жена же Лотова оглянулась позади
его и стала соляным столпом.
Книга Бытия

И праведник шел за посланником Бога,
Огромный и светлый, по черной горе.
Но громко жене говорила тревога:
Не поздно, ты можешь еще посмотреть

На красные башни родного Содома,
На площадь, где пела, на двор, где пряла
На окна пустые высокого дома,
Где милому мужу детей родила.

Взглянула, и, скованы смертною болью,
Глаза ее больше смотреть не могли;
И сделалось тело прозрачною солью,
И быстрые ноги к земле приросли.

Кто женщину эту оплакивать будет?
Не меньшей ли мнится она из утрат?
Лишь сердце мое никогда не забудет
Отдавшую жизнь за единственный взгляд.

24 февраля 1924

LOT'S WIFE

Lot's wife looked back from behind
him and became a pillar of salt.
Book of Genesis

And the righteous man followed the envoy of God,
Huge and bright, over the black mountain.
But anguish spoke loudly to his wife:
It is not too late, you can still gaze

At the red towers of your native Sodom,
At the square where you sang, at the courtyard where you spun,
At the empty windows of the tall house
Where you bore children to your beloved husband.

She glanced, and, paralyzed by deadly pain,
Her eyes no longer saw anything;
And her body became transparent salt
And her quick feet were rooted to the spot.

Who will weep for this woman?
Isn't her death the least significant?
But my heart will never forget the one
Who gave her life for a single glance.

February 24, 1924

МЕЛХОЛА

Но Давида полюбила...дочь Саулв,
Мелход. Саул думал: отдам ее за него, и она
будет ему сетью.

Первая Книга Царств

И отрок играет безумцу царю,
И ночь беспощадную рушит,
И громко победную кличет зарю,
И призраки ужаса душит.
И царь благосклонно ему говорит:
«Огонь в тебе, юноша, дивный горит,
И я за такое лекарство
Отдам тебе дочку и царство».
А царская дочка глядит на певца,
Ей песен не нужно, не нужно венца,
В душе ее скорбь и обида,
Но хочет Мелхола — Давида.
Бледнее, чем мертвая; рот ее сжат;
В зеленых глазах исступленье;
Сияют одежды, и стройно звенят
Запястья при каждом движенье.
Как тайна, как сон, как праматерь Лилит...
Не волей своею она говорит:
«Наверно, с отравой мне дали питье,
И мой помрачается дух,
Бесстыдство мое! Униженье мое!
Бродяга! Разбойник! Пастух!
Зачем же никто из придворных вельмож,
Увы, на него непохож?
А солнца лучи...а звезды в ночи...
А эта холодная дрожь...»

1959-1961

MICHAL

But David was loved … by the daughter of Saul,
Michal. Saul thought: I will give her to him, and
she will be a snare for him.
First Book of Kings

And the youth plays for the mad king,
And annihilates the merciless night,
And loudly summons triumphant dawn
And smothers the specters of fright.
And the king speaks kindly to him:
"In you, young man, burns a marvelous flame,
And for such a medicine
I will give you my daughter and my kingdom."
And the king's daughter stares at the singer,
She needs neither songs nor the marriage crown;
Her soul is full of grief and resentment,
Nevertheless, Michal wants David.
She is paler than death; her mouth is compressed,
In her green eyes, frenzy;
Her garments gleam and with each motion
Her bracelets ring harmoniously.
Like a mystery, like a dream, like the first mother, Lilith …
She speaks without volition:
"Surely they have given me drink with poison
And my spirit is clouded.
My shamelessness! My humiliation!
A vagabond! A brigand! A shepherd!
Why do none of the king's courtiers,
Alas, resemble him?
But the sun's rays … and the stars at night …
And this cold trembling …"

1959-1961

Наталии Рыковой

Все расхищено, предано, продано,
Черной смерти мелькало крыло,
Всё голодной тоскою изглодано,
Отчего же нам стало светло?

Днем дыханьями веет вишневыми
Небывалый под городом лес,
Ночью блещет созвездьями новыми
Глубь прозрачных июльских небес, —

И так близко подходит чудесное
К развалившимся грязным домам...
Никому, никому неизвестное,
Но от века желанное нам.

Июнь 1921

— to Natalya Rykova

Everything has been plundered, betrayed, sold out,
The wing of black death has flashed,
Everything has been devoured by starving anguish,
Why, then, is it so bright?

The fantastic woods near the town
Wafts the scent of cherry blossoms by day,
At night new constellations shine
In the transparent depths of the skies of July —

And how near the miraculous draws
To the dirty, tumbledown huts …
No one, no one knows what it is,
But for centuries we have longed for it.

June 1921

Страх, во тьме перебирая вещи,
Лунный луч наводит на топор.
За стеною слышен стук зловещий —
Что там, крысы, призрак или вор?

В душной кухне плещется водою,
Половицам шатким счет ведет,
С глянцевитой черной бородою
За окном чердачным промелькнет —

И притихнет. Как он зол и ловок,
Спички спрятал и свечу задул.
Лучше бы поблескиванье дул
В грудь мою направленных винтовок,

Лучше бы на площади зеленой
На помост некрашеный прилечь
И под клики радости и стоны
Красной кровью до конца истечь.

Прижимаю к сердцу крестик гладкий:
Боже, мир душе моей верни!
Запах тленья обморочно сладкий
Веет от прохладной простыни.

27-28 августа 1921
Царское Село

Terror, fingering things in the dark,
Leads the moonbeam to an ax.
Behind the wall there's an ominous knock —
What's there, a ghost, a thief, rats?

In the sweltering kitchen, water drips,
Counting the rickety floorboards.
Someone with a glossy black beard
flashes by the attic window —

And becomes still. How cunning he is and evil,
He hid the matches and blew out the candle.
How much better would be the gleam of the barrels
Of rifles leveled at my breast.

Better, in the grassy square,
To be flattened on the raw wood scaffold
And, amid cries of joy and moans,
Pour out my life's blood there.

I press the smooth cross to my heart:
God, restore peace to my soul.
The odor of decay, sickeningly sweet,
Rises from the clammy sheets.

August 27-28, 1921
Tsarskoye Selo

А Смоленская нынче именинница,
Синий ладан над травою стелется,
И струится пенье панихидное,
Не печальное нынче, а светлое.
И приводят румяные вдовушки
На кладбище мальчиков и девочек
Поглядеть на могилы отцовские,
А кладбище — роща соловьиная,
От сиянья солнечного замерло.
Принесли мы Смоленской Заступнице,
Принесли Пресвятой Богородице
На руках во гробе серебряном
Наше солнце, в муке погасшее —
Александра, лебедя чистого.

Август 1921

Today is the nameday of Our Lady of Smolensk,
Dark blue incense drifts over the grass,
And the flowing of the Requiem
Is no longer sorrowful, but radiant.
And the rosy little widows lead
Their boys and girls to the cemetery
To visit father's grave.
But the graveyard — a grove of nightingales,
Grows silent from the sun's bright blaze.
We have brought to the Intercessor of Smolensk,
We have brought to the Holy Mother of God,
In our hands in a silver coffin
Our sun, extinguished in torment —
Alexander, pure swan.

August 1921

ПРИЗРАК

Зажженных рано фонарей
Шары висячие скрежещут,
Всё праздничнее, всё светлей
Снежинки, пролетая, блещут.

И, ускоряя ровный бег,
Как бы в предчувствии погони,
Сквозь мягко падающий снег
Под синей сеткой мчатся кони.

И раззолоченный гайдук
Стоит недвижно за санями,
И странно царь глядит вокруг
Пустыми светлыми глазами.

Зима 1919

APPARITION

The round, hanging lanterns,
Lit early, are squeaking,
Ever more festively, ever brighter,
The flying snowflakes glitter.

And, quickening their steady gait,
As if sensing some pursuit,
Through the softly falling snow
Under a dark blue net, the horses race.

And the gilded footman
Stands motionless behind the sleigh,
And the tsar looks around strangely
With light, empty eyes.

Winter 1919

От тебя я сердце скрыла,
Словно бросила в Неву...
Прирученной и бескрылой
Я в дому твоем живу.
Только...ночью слышу скрипы,
Что там — в сумраках чужих?
Шереметевские липы...
Перекличка домовых...
Осторожно подступает
Как журчание воды;
К уху жарко приникает
Черный шепоток беды —
И бормочет, словно дело
Ей всю ночь возиться тут:
«Ты уюта захотела,
Знаешь, где он — твой уют?»

1936

I hid my heart from you
As if I had hurled it into the Neva …
Wingless and domesticated,
I live here in your home.
Only … at night I hear creaking.
What's there — in the strange gloom?
The Sheremetev lindens …
The roll call of the spirits of the house …
Approaching cautiously,
Like gurgling water,
Misfortune's black whisper
Nestles warmly to my ear —
And murmurs, as if this were
Its business for the night:
"You wanted comfort,
Do you know where it is — your comfort?"

1936

ПОЭТ

Он, сам себя сравнивший с конским глазом,
Косится, смотрит, видит, узнает,
И вот уже расплавленным алмазом
Сияют лужи, изнывает лед.

В лиловой мгле покоятся задворки,
Платформы, бревна, листья, облака.
Свист паровоза, хруст арбузной корки,
В душистой лайке робкая рука.

Звенит, гремит, скрежещет, бьет прибоем
И вдруг притихнет — это значит, он
Пугливо пробирается по хвоям,
Чтоб не спугнуть пространства чуткий сон.

И это значит, он считает зерна
В пустых колосьях, это значит, он
К плите дарьяльской, проклятой и черной,
Опять пришел с каких-то похорон.

И снова жжет московская истома,
Звенит вдали смертельный бубенец...
Кто заблудился в двух шагах от дома,
Где снег по пояс и всему конец?

THE POET

He who compared himself to the eye of a horse,
He glances sideways, looks, sees, recognizes,
And instantly puddles shine
As melted diamonds, ice pines.

In lilac haze repose backwards,
Station platforms, logs, leaves, clouds.
The whistle of a steam engine, the crunch of watermelon rind,
In a fragrant kid glove, a timid hand.

He rings out, thunders, grates, he beats like the surf
And suddenly grows quiet — it means that he
Is cautiously advancing through the pines,
So as not to disturb the light sleep of space.

And it means that he is counting the grains
From the stripped stalks, it means that he
Has come back to a Daryal gravestone, cursed and black,
After some kind of funeral.

And once more, Moscow weariness burns the throat,
Far off, a deadly little bell is ringing ...
Who lost his way two steps from the house,
Up to the waist in snow and no way out?

За то, что дым сравнил с Лаокооном,
Кладбищенский воспел чертополох,
За то, что мир наполнил новым звоном
В пространстве новом отраженных строф, —

Он награжден каким-то вечным детством,
Той щедростью и зоркостью светил,
И вся земля была его наследством,
А он ее со всеми разделил.

19 января 1936

Because he compared smoke to the Laocoön,
And celebrated cemetery thistles,
Because he filled the world with the new sound
Of his verse reverberating in new space —

He was rewarded with a kind of eternal childhood,
His generosity and keen-sightedness shone,
The whole earth was his inheritance,
And he shared it with everyone.

January 19, 1936

ВОРОНЕЖ

О.М.

И город весь стоит оледенелый.
Как под стеклом деревья, стены, снег.
По хрусталям я прохожу несмело.
Узорных санок так неверен бег.
А над Петром воронежским — вороны,
Да тополя, и свод светло-зеленый,
Размытый, мутный, в солнечной пыли,
И Куликовской битвой веют склоны
Могучей, победительной земли.
И тополя, как сдвинутые чаши,
Над нами сразу зазвенят сильней,
Как будто пьют за ликованье наше
На брачном пире тысячи гостей.

А в комнате опального поэта
Дежурят страх и Муза в свой черед.
И ночь идет,
Которая не ведает рассвета.

4 марта 1936

VORONEZH

O. M.

And the whole town is encased in ice,
Trees, walls, snow, as if under glass.
Timidly, I walk on crystals,
Gaily painted sleds skid.
And over the Peter of Voronezh — crows,
Poplar trees, and the dome, light green,
Faded, dulled, in sunny haze,
And the battle of Kulikovo blows from the slopes
Of the mighty, victorious land.
And the poplars, like cups clashed together,
Roar over us, stronger and stronger,
As if our joy were toasted by
A thousand guests at a wedding feast.

But in the room of the poet in disgrace,
Fear and the Muse keep watch by turns.
And the night comes on
That knows no dawn.

March 4, 1936

Привольем пахнет дикий мед.
Пыль — солнечным лучом,
Фиалкою — девичий рот,
А золото — ничем.
Водою пахнет резеда,
И яблоком — любовь.
Но мы узнали навсегда,
Что кровью пахнет только кровь...

И напрасно наместник Рима
Мыл руки пред всем народом,
Под зловещие крики черни;
И шотландская королева
Напрасно с узких ладоней
Стирала красные брызги
В душном мраке царского дома...

1933

Wild honey smells like freedom,
Dust — like a ray of sun.
Like violets — a young maid's mouth,
And gold — like nothing.
The flowers of the mignonette smell like water,
And like an apple — love.
But we learned once and for all
That blood smells only like blood …

And in vain the vice-regent of Rome
Washed his hands before all the people,
Urged on by the ominous shouts of the rabble;
And the Scottish queen
In vain washed the spattered red drops
From her slender palms
In the stifling gloom of the king's home …

1933

РЕКВИЕМ

Нет, и не под чуждым небосводом,
И не под защитой чуждых крыл, —
Я была тогда с моим народом,
Там, где мой народ, к несчастью, был.

1961

ВМЕСТО ПРЕДИСЛОВИЯ

В страшные годы ежовщины я провела семнадцать месяцев в тюремных очередях в Ленинграде. Как-то раз кто-то «опознал» меня. Тогда стоящая за мной женщина с голубыми губами, которая,конечно, никогда в жизни не слыхала моего имени, очнулась от свойственного нам всем оцепенения и спросила меня на ухо (там все говорили шепотом):

—А это вы можете описать?

И я сказала:

—Могу.

Тогда что-то вроде улыбки скользнуло по тому, что некогда было ее лицом.

1 апреля 1957 г.
Ленинград

REQUIEM

No, not under the vault of alien skies,
And not under the shelter of alien wings —
I was with my people then,
There, where my people, unfortunately, were.

1961

INSTEAD OF A PREFACE

In the terrible years of the Yezhov terror, I spent seventeen months in the prison lines of Leningrad. Once, someone "recognized" me. Then a woman with bluish lips standing behind me, who, of course, had never heard me called by name before, woke up from the stupor to which everyone had succumbed and whispered in my ear (everyone spoke in whispers there):

"Can you describe this?"

And I answered: "Yes, I can."

Then something that looked like a smile passed over what had once been her face.

April 1, 1957
Leningrad

ПОСВЯЩЕНИЕ

Перед этим горем гнутся горы,
Не течет великая река,
Но крепки тюремные затворы,
А за ними «каторжные норы»
И смертельная тоска.
Для кого-то веет ветер свежий,
Для кого-то нежится закат —
Мы не знаем, мы повсюду те же,
Слышим лишь ключей постылый скрежет
Да шаги тяжелые солдат.
Подымались как к обедне ранней,
По столице одичалой шли,
Там встречались, мертвых бездыханней,
Солнце ниже и Нева туманней,
А надежда все поет вдали.
Приговор...И сразу слезы хлынут,
Ото всех уже отделена,
Словно с болью жизнь из сердца вынут,
Словно грубо навзничь опрокинут,
Но идет...Шатается...Одна...
Где теперь невольные подруги
Двух моих осатанелых лет?
Что им чудится в сибирской вьюге,
Что мерещится им в лунном круге?
Им я шлю прощальный свой привет.

Март 1940 г.

DEDICATION

Mountains bow down to this grief,
Mighty rivers cease to flow,
but the prison gates hold firm,
And behind them are the "prisoners' burrows"
And mortal woe.
For someone a fresh breeze blows,
For someone the sunset luxuriates —
We wouldn't know, we are those who everywhere
Hear only the rasp of the hateful key
And the soldiers' heavy tread.
We rose as if for an early service,
trudged through the savaged capital
And met there, more lifeless than the dead;
The sun is lower and the Neva mistier,
But hope keeps singing from afar.
The verdict … And her tears gush forth,
Already she is cut off from the rest,
as if they painfully wrenched life from her heart,
As if they brutally knocked her flat,
But she goes on … Staggering … Alone …
Where now are my chance friends
Of those two diabolical years?
What do they imagine is in Siberia's storms,
What appears to them dimly in the circle of the moon?
I am sending my farewell greeting to them.

March 1940

ВСТУПЛЕНИЕ

Это было, когда улыбался
Только мертвый, спокойствию рад.
И ненужным привеском болтался
Возле тюрем своих Ленинград.
И когда, обезумев от муки,
Шли уже осужденных полки,
И короткую песню разлуки
Паровозные пели гудки.
Звезды смерти стояли над нами,
И безвинная корчилась Русь
Под кровавыми сапогами
И под шинами черных марусь.

I

Уводили тебя на рассвете,
За тобой, как на выносе, шла,
В темной горнице плакали дети,
У божницы свеча оплыла.
На губах твоих холод иконки,
Смертный пот на челе...Не забыть! —
Буду я, как стрелецкие женки,
Под кремлевскими башнями выть.

1935 г.
Москва

PROLOGUE

That was when the ones who smiled
Were the dead, glad to be at rest.
And like a useless appendage, Leningrad
Swung from its prisons.
And when, senseless from torment,
Regiments of convicts marched,
And the short songs of farewell
Were sung by locomotive whistles.
The stars of death stood above us
And innocent Russia writhed
Under bloody boots
And under the tires of the Black Marias.

I

They led you away at dawn,
I followed you, like a mourner,
In the dark front room the children were crying,
By the icon shelf the candle was dying.
On your lips was the icon's chill.
The deathly sweat on your brow … Unforgettable! —
I will be like the wives of the Streltsy,
Howling under the Kremlin towers.

1935
Moscow

II

Тихо льется тихий Дон,
Желтый месяц входит в дом.

Входит в шапке набекрень,
Видит желтый месяц тень.

Эта женщина больна,
Эта женщина одна.

Муж в могиле, сын в тюрьме,
Помолитесь обо мне.

III

Нет, это не я, это кто-то другой страдает.
Я бы так не могла, а то, что случилось,
Пусть черные сукна покроют,
И пусть унесть фонари...
                                        Ночь.

1940

II

Quietly flows the quiet Don,
Yellow moon slips into a home.

He slips in with cap askew,
He sees a shadow, yellow moon.

This woman is ill,
This woman is alone,

Husband in the grave, son in prison,
Say a prayer for me.

III

No, it is not I, it is somebody else who is suffering.
I would not have been able to bear what happened,
Let them shroud it in black,
And let them carry off the lanterns …
                    Night.

1940

IV

Показать бы тебе, насмешнице
И любимице всех друзей,
Царскосельской веселой грешнице,
Что случится с жизнью твоей —
Как трехсотая, с передачею,
Под Крестами будешь стоять
И своею слезой горячею
Новогодний лед прожигать.
Там тюремный тополь качается,
И ни звука — а сколько там
Неповинных жизней кончается...

V

Семнадцать месяцев кричу,
Зову тебя домой,
Кидалась в ноги палачу,
Ты сын и ужас мой.
Все перепуталось навек,
И мне не разобрать
Теперь, кто зверь, кто человек,
И долго ль казни ждать.
И только пышные цветы,
Куда-то в никуда.
И прямо мне в глаза глядит
И скорой гибелью грозит
Огромная звезда.

1939

IV

You should have been shown, you mocker,
Minion of all your friends,
Gay little sinner of Tsarskoye Selo,
What would happen in your life —
How three-hundredth in line, with a parcel,
You would stand by the Kresty prison,
Your fiery tears
Burning through the New Year's ice.
Over there the prison poplar bends,
And there's no sound — and over there how many
innocent lives are ending now …

V

For seventeen months I've been crying out,
Calling you home.
I flung myself at the hangman's feet,
You are my son and my horror.
Everything is confused forever,
And it's not clear to me
Who is a beast now, who is a man,
And how long before the execution.
And there are only dusty flowers,
And the chinking of the censer, and tracks
From somewhere to nowhere.
And staring me straight in the eyes,
And threatening impending death,
Is an enormous star.

1939

VI

Легкие летят недели.
Что случилось, не пойму,
Как тебе, сынок, в тюрьму
Ночи белые глядели,
Как они опять глядят
Ястребиным жарким оком,
О твоем кресте высоком
И о смерти говорят.

Весна 1939 г.

VII
ПРИГОВОР

И упало каменное слово
На мою еще живую грудь.
Ничего, ведь я была готова,
Справлюсь с этим как-нибудь.

У меня сегодня много дела:
Надо память до конца убить,
Надо, чтоб душа окаменела,
Надо снова научится жить.

А не то...Горячий шелест лета,
Словно праздник за моим окном.
Я давно предчувствовала этот
Светлый день и опустелый дом.

22 июня 1939 г.
Фонтанный Дом

VI

The light weeks will take flight,
I won't comprehend what happened.
Just as the white nights
Stared at you, dear son, in prison,
So they are staring again,
With the burning eyes of a hawk,
Talking about your lofty cross,
And about death.

Spring 1939

VII
THE SENTENCE

And the stone word fell
On my still-living breast.
Never mind, I was ready.
I will manage somehow.

Today I have so much to do:
I must kill memory once and for all,
I must turn my soul to stone,
I must learn to live again —

Unless … Summer's ardent rustling
Is like a festival outside my window.
For a long time I've foreseen this
Brilliant day, deserted house.

June 22, 1939
Fountain House

VIII
К СМЕРТИ

Ты все равно придешь — зачем же не теперь?
Я жду тебя — мне очень трудно.
Я потушила свет и отворила дверь
Тебе, такой простой и чудной.
Прими для этого какой угодно вид,
Ворвись отравленным снарядом
Иль с гирькой подкрадись, как опытный бандит,
Иль отрави тифозным чадом.
Иль сказочкой, придуманной тобой
И всем до тошноты знакомой, —
Чтоб я увидела верх шапки голубой
И бледного от страха управдома.
Мне все равно теперь. Клубится Енисей,
Звезда Полярная сияет.
И синий блеск возлюбленных очей
Последний ужас застилает.

19 августа 1939 г.
Фонтанный Дом

VIII
TO DEATH

You will come in any case — so why not now?
I am waiting for you — I can't stand much more.
I've put out the light and opened the door
For you, so simple and miraculous.
So come in any form you please,
Burst in as a gas shell
Or, like a gangster, steal in with a length of pipe,
Or poison me with typhus fumes.
Or be that fairy tale you've dreamed up,
So sickeningly familiar to everyone —
In which I glimpse the top of a pale blue cap
And the house attendant white with fear.
Now it doesn't matter anymore. The Yenisey swirls,
The North Star shines.
And the final horror dims
The blue luster of beloved eyes.

August 19, 1939
Fountain House

IX

Уже безумие крылом
Души накрыло половину,
И поит огненным вином
И манит в черную долину.

И поняла я, что ему
Должна я уступить победу,
Прислушиваясь к своему
Уже как бы чужому бреду.

И не позволит ничего
Оно мне унести с собою
(Как ни упрашивай его
И как ни докучай мольбою):

Ни сына страшные глаза —
Окаменелое страданье, —
Ни день, когда пришла гроза,
Ни час тюремного свиданья,

Ни милую прохладу рук,
Ни лип взволнованные тени,
Ни отдаленный легкий звук —
Слова последних утешений.

4 мая 1940 г.
Фонтанный Дом

IX

Now madness half shadows
My soul with its wing,
And makes it drunk with fiery wine
And beckons toward the black ravine.

And I've finally realized
That I must give in,
Overhearing myself
Raving as if it were somebody else.

And it does not allow me to take
Anything of mine with me
(No matter how I plead with it,
No matter how I supplicate):

Not the terrible eyes of my son —
Suffering turned to stone,
Not the day of the terror,
Not the hour I met with him in prison,

Not the sweet coolness of his hands,
Not the trembling shadow of the lindens,
Not the far-off, fragile sound —
Of the final words of consolation.

May 4, 1940
Fountain House

X

РАСПЯТИЕ

«Не рыдай Мене, Мати,
во гробе сущу»

1

Хор ангелов великий час восславил,
И небеса расплавились в огне.
Отцу сказал: «Почто Меня оставил!
А Матери: «О, не рыдай Мене...»

1940
Фонтанный Дом

2

Магдалина билась и рыдала,
Ученик любимый каменел,
А туда, где молча Мать стояла,
Так никто взглянуть и не посмел.

1943
Ташкент

X

CRUCIFIXION

"Do not weep for Me, Mother,
I am in the grave."

1

A choir of angels sang the praises of that momentous hour,
And the heavens dissolved in fire.
To his Father He said: "Why hast Thou forsaken me!"
And to his Mother: "Oh, do not weep for Me … "

1940
Fountain House

2

Mary Magdalene beat her breast and sobbed,
The beloved disciple turned to stone,
But where the silent Mother stood, there
No one glanced and no one would have dared.

1943
Tashkent

ЭПИЛОГ I

Узнала я, как опадают лица,
Как из-под век выглядывает страх,
Как клинописи жесткие страницы
Страдание выводит на щеках,
Как локоны из пепельных и черных
Серебряными делаются вдруг,
Улыбка вянет на губах покорных,
И в сухоньком смешке дрожит испуг.
И я молюсь не о себе одной,
А обо всех, кто там стоял со мною,
И в лютый холод, и в июльский зной
Под красною, ослепшею стеною.

II

Опять поминальный приблизился час.
Я вижу, я слышу, я чувствую вас:

И ту, что едва до окна довели,
И ту, что родимой не топчет земли,

И ту, что красивой тряхнув головой,
Сказала: «Сюда прихожу, как домой».

Хотелось бы всех поименно назвать,
Да отняли список, и негде узнать.

Для них соткала я широкий покров
Из бедных, у них же подслушанных слов.

EPILOGUE I

I learned how faces fall,
How terror darts from under eyelids,
How suffering traces lines
Of stiff cuneiform on cheeks,
How locks of ashen-blonde or black
Turn silver suddenly,
Smiles fade on submissive lips
And fear trembles in a dry laugh.
And I pray not for myself alone,
But for all those who stood there with me
In cruel cold, and in July's heat,
At that blind, red wall.

EPILOGUE II

Once more the day of remembrance draws near.
I see, I hear, I feel you:

The one they almost had to drag at the end,
And the one who tramps her native land no more,

And the one who, tossing her beautiful head,
Said: "Coming here's like coming home."

I'd like to name them all by name,
But the list has been confiscated and is nowhere to be found.

I have woven a wide mantle for them
From their meager, overheard words.

О них вспоминаю всегда и везде,
О них не забуду и в новой беде,

И если зажмут мой измученный рот,
Которым кричит стомильонный народ,

Пусть так же они поминают меня
В канун моего поминального дня.

А если когда-нибудь в этой стране
Воздвигнуть задумают памятник мне,

Согласье на это даю торжество,
Но только с условьем — не ставить его

Ни около моря, где я родилась:
Последняя с морем разорвана связь,

Ни в царском саду у заветного пня,
Где тень безутешная ищет меня,

А здесь, где стояла я триста часов
И где для меня не открыли засов.

Затем, что и в смерти блаженной боюсь
Забыть громыхание черных марусь,

Забыть, как постылая хлопала дверь
И выла старуха, как раненый зверь.

И пусть с неподвижных и бронзовых век
Как слезы, струится подтаявший снег,

И голубь тюремный пусть гулит вдали,
И тихо идут по Неве корабли.

марта 1940 г.

I will remember them always and everywhere,
I will never forget them no matter what comes.

And if they gag my exhausted mouth
Through which a hundred million scream,

Then may the people remember me
On the eve of my remembrance day.

And if ever in this country
They decide to erect a monument to me,

I consent to that honor
Under these conditions — that it stand

Neither by the sea, where I was born:
My last tie with the sea is broken,

Nor in the tsar's garden near the cherished pine stump,
Where an inconsolable shade looks for me,

But here, where I stood for three hundred hours,
And where they never unbolted the doors for me.

This, lest in blissful death
I forget the rumbling of the Black Marias,

Forget how that detested door slammed shut
And an old woman howled like a wounded animal.

And may the melting snow stream like tears
From my motionless lids of bronze,

And a prison dove coo in the distance,
And the ships of the Neva sail calmly on.

March 1940

КЛЕОПАТРА

Александрийские чертоги
Покрыла сладостная тень.
Пушкин

Уже целовала Антония мертвые губы,
Уже на коленях пред Августом слезы лила
И предали слуги. Грохочут победные трубы...
Под римским орлом, и вечерняя стелется мгла.
И входит последний плененный ее красотою,
Высокий и статный, и шепчет в смятении он:
«Тебя — как рабыню... в триумфе пошлет пред собою...»
Но шеи лебяжьей все так же спокоен наклон.

А завтра детей закуют. О, как мало осталось
Ей дела на свете — еще с мужиком пошутить
И черную змейку, как будто прощальную жалость,
На смуглую грудь равнодушной рукой положить.

7 февраля 1940

CLEOPATRA

Alexandria's palaces
Were covered with sweet shade.
Pushkin

She had already kissed Antony's dead lips,
And on her knees before Augustus had poured out
her tears …
And the servants betrayed her. Victorious trumpets blare
Under the Roman eagle, and the mist of evening drifts.
Then enters the last captive of her beauty,
Tall and grave, and he whispers in embarrassment:
"You — like a slave … will be led before him in
the triumph …"
But the swan's neck remains peacefully inclined.

And tomorrow they'll put the children in chains. Oh,
how little remains
For her to do on earth — joke a little with this boy
And, as if in a valedictory gesture of compassion,
Place the black viper on her dusky breast with an
indifferent hand.

February 7, 1940

ДАНТЕ

Il mio bel San Giovanni.
Dante

Он и после смерти не вернулся
В старую Флоренцию свою.
Этот, уходя, не оглянулся,
Этому я эту песнь пою.
Факел, ночь, последнее объятье,
За порогом дикий вопль судьбы.
Он из ада ей послал проклятье
И в раю не мог ее забыть, —
Но босой, в рубахе покаянной,
Со свечой зажженной не прошел
По своей Флоренции желанной,
Вероломной, низкой, долгожданной...

17 августа 1936

DANTE

Il mio bel San Giovanni.
Dante

Even after his death he did not return
To his ancient Florence.
To the one who, leaving, did not look back,
To him I sing this song.
A torch, the night, the last embrace,
Beyond the threshold, the wild wail of fate.
From hell he sent her curses
And in paradise he could not forget her —
But barefoot, in a hair shirt,
With a lighted candle he did not walk
Through his florence — his beloved,
Perfidious, base, longed for …

August 17, 1936

ПОСЛЕДНИЙ ТОСТ

Я пью за разоренный дом,
За злую жизнь мою,
За одиночество вдвоем
И за тебя я пью, —
За ложь меня предавших губ,
За мертвый холод глаз,
За то, что мир жесток и груб,
За то, что Бог не спас.

27 июня 1934

THE LAST TOAST

I drink to the ruined house,
To the evil of my life,
To our shared loneliness
And I drink to you —
To the lie of lips that betrayed me,
To the deadly coldness of the eyes,
To the fact that the world is cruel and depraved,
To the fact that God did not save.

June 27, 1934

МАЯКОВСКИЙ В 1913 ГОДУ

Я тебя в твоей не знала славе,
Помню только бурный твой рассвет,
Но, быть может, я сегодня вправе
Вспомнить день тех отдаленных лет.
Как в стихах твоих крепчали звуки,
Новые роились голоса...
Не ленились молодые руки,
Грозные ты возводил леса.
Всё, чего касался ты, казалось
Не таким, как было до тех пор,
То, что разрушал ты,— разрушалось,
В каждом слове бился приговор.
Одинок и часто недоволен,
С нетерпеньем торопил судьбу,
Знал, что скоро выйдешь весел, волен
На свою великую борьбу.
И уже отзывный гул прилива
Слышался, когда ты нам читал,
Дождь косил свои глааа гневливо,
С городом ты в буйный спор вступал.
И еше не слышанное имя
Молнией влетело в душный зал,
Чтобы ныне, всей страной хранимо,
Зазвучать, как боевой сигнал.

8-10 марта 1940

MAYAKOVSKY IN 1913

I didn't know you in your glory,
I only remember your stormy dawn.
But perhaps today I have the right
To recall a day from those far-off years.
How in your poems sounds hardened,
New voices swarmed ...
Your youthful hands were not lying idle,
You were constructing formidable scaffolding.
Everything you touched no longer seemed
The same as it had been before.
What you destroyed — was destroyed,
A verdict beat in every word.
Lonely and often dissatisfied,
You rushed your fate impatiently,
You knew that soon, joyful and free,
You would begin your great battle.
And the hum of the rising tide of response
Was audible as you read to us.
Rain slanted its eyes wrathfully,
You quarreled violently with the city.
And your still unheralded name
flew like lightning around the stuffy hall,
So that today, treasured throughout the land,
It might ring out like a battle-cry.

March 8-10, 1940

Вспыхнул над молом первый маяк,
Других маяков предтеча, —
Заплакал и шапку снял моряк,
Что плавал в набитых смертью морях
Вдоль смерти и смерти навстречу.

1942-45

The first lighthouse flashed over the jetty,
The precursor of many —
And the sailor who had sailed seas packed with death,
Alongside death and on the way to death,
Took off his cap and wept.

1942-45

ТВОРЧЕСТВО

Бывает так: какая-то истома;
В ушах не умолкает бой часов;
Вдали раскат стихающего грома.
Неузнанных и пленных голосов
Мне чудятся и жалобы и стоны,
Сужается какой-то тайный круг,
Но в этой бездне шепотов и звонов
Встает один, всё победивший звук.
Так вкруг него непоправимо тихо,
Что слышно, как в лесу растет трава,
Как по земле идет с котомкой лихо...
Но вот уже послышались слова
И легких рифм сигнальные звоночки, —
Тогда я начинаю понимать,
И просто продиктованные строчки
Ложатся в белоснежную тетрадь.

5 ноября 1936
Фонтанный Дом

CREATION

It happens like this: a kind of languor;
A ceaseless striking of a clock is heard;
Far off, a dying peal of thunder.
I somehow sense the groaning and the sorrows
Of unrecognized, imprisoned voices,
A kind of secret circle narrows;
But in the abyss of whispers and ringing
Rises one triumphant sound.
Such an absolute silence surrounds it
That one can hear the grass growing in the woods,
How misfortune with a knapsack plods the earth . . .
But now words are beginning to be heard
And the signaling chimes of light rhymes —
Then I begin to comprehend,
And the simply dictated lines
Lie down in place on the snow-white page.

November 5, 1936
Fountain House

2

Мне ни к чему одические рати
И прелесть элегических затей.
По мне, в стихах все быть должно некстати,
Не так, как у людей.

Когда б вы знали, из какого сора
Растут стихи, не ведая стыда,
Как желтый одуванчик у забора,
Как лопухи и лебеда.

Сердитый окрик, дегтя запах свежий,
Таинственная плесень на стене...
И стих уже звучит, задорен, нежен,
На радость вам и мне.

21 января 1940

10

Многое еще, наверно, хочет
Быть воспетым голосом моим:
То, что, бессловесное, грохочет,
Иль во тьме подземный камень точит,
Или пробивается сквозь дым.
У меня не выяснены счеты
С пламенем, и ветром, и водой...
Оттого-то мне мои дремоты
Вдруг такие распахнут ворота
И ведут за утренней звездой.

1942
Ташкент

2

I don't need martial hosts arrayed in odes
And the charm of ornamental elegies.
For me, everything in poetry should be out of place,
Not what people think it is.

If only you knew from what rubbish
Poetry grows, knowing no shame,
Like a yellow dandelion by the fence,
Like burdock and goosefoot.

An angry cry, fresh smell of tar,
Mysterious mold on the wall . . .
And suddenly a line rings out, lively, tender,
To my delight and yours.

January 21, 1940

10

Probably much still remains
To be celebrated by my voice:
That which, wordless, rumbles around,
Or in darkness grinds stone underground,
Or makes its way through smoke.
I haven't yet closed my accounts
With flame and wind and water . . .
Because of that, my drowsiness
Suddenly flings wide such gates to me
And leads beyond the morning star.

1942
Tashkent

ПАМЯТИ ДРУГА

И в День Победы, нежный и туманный,
Когда заря, как зарево, красна,
Вдовою у могилы безымянной
Хлопочет запоздалая весна.
Она с холен подняться не спешит,
Дохнет на почку и траву погладит,
И бабочку с плеча на землю ссадит,
И первый одуванчик распушит.

8 ноября 1945

TO THE MEMORY OF A FRIEND

And on this Day of Victory, tender and misty,
When dawn is as red as the fire's glow,
Like a widow at a nameless grave,
The late spring keeps fidgeting about.
She is not in a hurry to rise from her knees,
She breathes on a bud and smoothes the lawn,
And helps a butterfly from her shoulder to the ground,
And fluffs up the first dandelion.

November 8, 1945

Я не была здесь лет семьсот,
Но ничего не изменилось...
Всё так же льется божья милость
С непререкаемых высот,

Всё те же хоры звезд и вод,
Всё так же своды неба черны,
И так же ветер носит зерна,
И ту же песню мать поет.

Он прочен, мой азийский дом,
И беспокоиться не надо...
Еще приду. Цвети, ограда,
Будь полон, чистый водоем.

5 мая 1944

I haven't been here for seven hundred years,
But nothing has changed ...
In the same way the grace of God still pours
From unassailable heights,

The same choirs of stars and water,
The same black vaults of sky,
And the wind spreads the seed the same way,
And mother sings the same song.

My Asian house is sound,
And I can be tranquil ...
I will return. And now, fence, bloom!
New reservoir, fill!

May 5, 1944

Когда лежит луна ломтем чарджуйской дыни
На краешке окна и духота кругом,
Когда закрыта дверь, и заколдован дом
Воз душной веткой голубых глициний,
И в чашке глиняной холодная вода,
И полотенца снег, и свечка восковая
Горит, как в детстве, мотыльков сзывая,
Грохочет тишина, моих не слыша слов,—
Тогда из черноты рембрандтовских углов
Склубится что-то вдруг и спрячется туда же,
Но я не встрепенусь, не испугаюсь даже...
Здесь одиночество меня поймало в сети.
Хозяйкин черный кот глядит, как глаз столетий,
И в зеркале двойник не хочет мне помочь.
Я буду сладко спать. Спокойной ночи, ночь».

29 марта 1944
Ташкент

When the moon lies like a slice of Chardush melon
On the windowsill and it's hard to breathe,
When the door is shut and the house bewitched
By an airy branch of blue wisteria,
And there is cool water in the clay cup,
And a snow-white towel, and the wax candle
Is burning, as in my childhood, attracting moths,
The silence roars, not hearing my words —
Then from corners black as Rembrandt's
Something rears and hides itself again,
But I won't rouse myself, won't even take fright …
Here loneliness has caught me in its net.
The landlady's black cat stares like the eye of centuries,
And the double in the mirror doesn't want to help me.
I will sleep sweetly. Good night, night.

March 28, 1944
Tashkent

Это рысьи глаза твои, Азия,
Что-то высмотрели во мне,
Что-то выдразнили подспудное
И рожденное тишиной,
И томительное, и трудное,
Как полдневный термезский зной.
Словно вся прапамять в сознание
Раскаленной лавой текла,
Словно я свои же рыдания
Из чужих ладоней пила.

1945

Those lynx eyes of yours, Asia,
Spied out something in me,
Teased out something latent
And born of silence,
And oppressive, and as difficult to bear
As the noonday heat of Termez.
It was as if into my consciousness all of pre-memory
Like molten lava poured,
As if I were drinking my own sobs
From a stranger's palms.

1945

CINQUE

Autant que toi sans doute il te sera fidèle
Et constant jusques à la mort.
—Baudelaire

1

Как у облака на краю,
Вспоминаю я речь твою,

А тебе от речи моей
Стали ночи светлее дней.

Так, отторгнутые от земли,
Высоко мы, как звезды, шли.

Ни отчаянья, ни стыда
Ни теперь, ни потом, ни тогда.

Но живого и наяву,
Слышишь ты, как тебя зову.

И ту дверь, что ты приоткрыл,
Мне захлопнуть не хватит сил.

26 ноября 1945

CINQUE

Autant que toi sans doute il te sera fidèle
Et constant jusques à la mort.
—Baudelaire

1

As if on the rim of a cloud,
I remember your words,

And because of my words to you,
Night became brighter than day.

Thus, torn from the earth,
We rose up, like stars.

There was neither despair nor shame,
Not now, not afterward, not at the time.

But in real life, right now,
You hear how I am calling you.

And that door that you half opened,
I don't have the strength to slam.

November 26, 1945

2

Истлевают звуки в эфире,
И заря притворилась тьмой.
В навсегда онемевшем мире
Два лишь голоса: твой и мой.
И под ветер с незримых Ладог,
Сквозь почти колокольный звон,
В легкий блеск перекрестных радуг
Разговор ночной превращен.

20 декабря 1945

3

Я не любила с давних дней,
Чтобы меня жалели,
А с каплей жалости твоей
Иду, как с солнцем в теле.
Вот от отчего вокруг заря.
Иду я, чудеса творя,
Вот отчего!

20 декабря 1945

2

Sounds die away in the ether,
And darkness overtakes the dusk.
In a world become mute for all time,
There are only two voices: yours and mine.
And to the almost bell-like sound
Of the wind from invisible Lake Ladoga,
That late-night dialogue turned into
The delicate shimmer of interlaced rainbows.

December 20, 1945

3

For so long I hated
To be pitied,
But one drop of your pity
And I go around as if the sun were in my body.
That's why there is dawn all around me.
I go around creating miracles,
That's why!

December 20, 1945

4

Знаешь сам, что не стану славить
Нашей встречи горчайший день.
Что тебе на память оставить,
Тень мою? На что тебе тень?
Посвященье сожженной драмы,
От которой и пепла нет,
Или вышедший вдруг из рамы
Новогодний страшный портрет?
Или слышимый еле-еле
Звон березовых угольков,
Или то, что мне не успели
Досказать про чужую любовь?

6 января 1946

5

Не дышали мы сонными маками,
И своей мы не знаем вины.
Под какими же звездными знаками
Мы на горе себе рождены?

И какое кромешное варево
Поднесла нам январская тьма?
И какое незримое зарево
Нас до света сводило с ума?

11 января 1946

4

You know yourself that I'm not going to celebrate
The most bitter day of our meeting.
What to leave you in remembrance?
My shade? What good is a ghost to you?
The dedication to a burnt drama
Of which not an ash remains,
Or the terrible New Year's portrait
Suddenly hurled from its frame.
Or the barely audible
Sound of birch embers.
Or that they didn't have time to tell me of
Another's love.

January 6, 1946

5

We hadn't breathed the poppies' somnolence,
And we ourselves don't know our sin.
What was in our stars
That destined us for sorrow?

And what kind of hellish brew
Did the January darkness bring us?
And what kind of invisible glow
Drove us out of our minds before dawn?

January 11, 1946

СОЖЖЕННАЯ ТЕТРЯДЬ

Уже красуется на книжной полке
Твоя благополучная сестра,
А над тобою звездных стай осколки
И под тобою угольки костра.
Как ты молила, как ты жить хотела,
Как ты боялась едкого огня!
Но вдруг твое затрепетало тело,
А голос, улетая, клял меня.
И сразу все зашелестели сосны
И отразились в недрах лунных вод.
А вкруг костра священнейшие весны
Уже вели надгробный хоровод.

1961

THE BURNT NOTEBOOK

On the bookshelf standing in splendor
Is your prosperous sister,
But over you are the shards of flocks of stars,
And under you the coals of a fire.
How you prayed, how you wanted to live,
How you feared the acrid flame!
But suddenly your body began to flutter,
And your voice, flying off, cursed me.
And at once the pines began to rustle
And were reflected in the depths of the moonlit water.
And already the most sacred springtime
Led the funeral dance around the fire.

1961

Ты выдумал меня. Такой на свете нет,
Такой на свете быть не может.
Ни врач не исцелит, ни утолит поэт, —
Тень призрака тебя и день и ночь тревожит.
Мы встретились с тобой в невероятный год,
Когда уже иссякли мира силы,
Все было в трауре, все никло от невзгод,
И были свежи лишь могилы.
Без фонарей как смоль был черен невский вал,
Глухая ночь вокруг стеной стояла...
Так вот когда тебя мой голос вызывал!
Что делала — сама еще не понимала.
И ты пришел ко мне, как бы звездой ведом,
По осени трагической ступая,
В тот навсегда опустошенный дом,
Откуда унеслась стихов сожженных стая.

18 августа 1956
Старки

You invented me. There is no such earthly being,
Such an earthly being there could never be.
A doctor cannot cure, a poet cannot comfort —
A shadowy apparition haunts you night and day.
We met in an unbelievable year,
When the world's strength was at an ebb,
Everything was in mourning, everything withered by adversity,
And only the graves were fresh.
Without streetlights, the Neva's waves were black as pitch,
Thick night enclosed me like a wall …
That's when my voice called out to you!
Why it did — I still don't understand.
And you came to me, as if guided by a star
That tragic autumn, stepping
Into that irrevocably ruined house,
From whence had flown a flock of burnt verse.

August 18, 1956
Starky

Против воли я твой, царица,
берег покинул.

Энеида, Песнь 6.

Не пугайся, — я еще похожей
Нас теперь изобразить могу.
Призрак ты — иль человек прохожий,
Тень твою зачем-то берегу.

Был недолго ты моим Энеем, —
Я тогда отделалась костром.
Друг о друге мы молчать умеем.
И забыл ты мой проклятый дом.

Ты забыл те, в ужасе и в муке,
Сквозь огонь протянутые руки
И надежды окаянной весть.

Ты не знаешь, что́ тебе простили...
Создан Рим, плывут стада флотилий,
И победу славословит лесть.

1962
Комарово

I abandoned your shores, Empress,
against my will.
Aeneid, Book 6

Don't be afraid — I can still portray
What we resemble now.
You are a ghost — or a man passing through,
And for some reason I cherish your shade.

For a while you were my Aeneas —
It was then I escaped by fire.
We know how to keep quiet about one another.
And you forgot my cursed house.

You forgot those hands stretched out to you
In horror and torment, through flame,
And the report of blasted dreams.

You don't know for what you were forgiven …
Rome was created, flocks of flotillas sail on the sea,
And adulation sings the praises of victory.

1962
Komarovo

ЕЩЕ ТОСТ

За веру твою! И за верность мою!
За то, что с тобою мы в этом краю!
Пускай навсегда заколдованы мы,
Но не было в мире прекрасней зимы,
И не было в небе узорней крестов,
Воздушней цепочек, длиннее мостов...
За то, что все плыло, беззвучно скользя.
За то, что нам видеть друг друга нельзя.
За то, что мне сниться еще и теперь,
Хоть прочно туда заколочена дверь.

1961-1963

ONE MORE TOAST

To your faith! And to my faithfulness!
Because we're together in this land!
Let us remain bewitched forever,
For never was a winter in the world more beautiful,
And never in the sky were there more delicate crosses,
Longer bridges, more airy chains …
Because everything is floating, silently gliding.
Because it's impossible to see one another again.
Because I'm dreaming about it
Even though the door is nailed shut.

1961-63

ПРИМОРСКИЙ СОНЕТ

Здесь все меня переживет,
Все, даже ветхие скворешни
И этот воздух, воздух вешний,
Морской свершивший перелет.

И голос вечности зовет
С неодолимостью нездешней,
И над цветущею черешней
Сиянье легкий месяц льет.

И кажется такой нетрудной,
Белея в чаще изумрудной,
Дорога не скажу куда...

Там средь стволов еще светлее,
И все похоже на аллею
У царскосельского пруда.

Июнь 1958
Комарово

SEASIDE SONNET

Here everything will outlive me,
Everything, even the decrepit starling houses,
And this breeze, a vernal breeze,
finishing its flight from across the sea.

And the voice of eternity beckons
With unearthly irresistibility,
And over the blossoming cherry trees
The crescent moon pours radiance.

And it seems so clear,
Growing white in the emerald underbrush,
The road to — I won't say where ...

There among the tree trunks it's brighter still,
And everything resembles the allée
Along the pond at Tsarskoe Selo.

June 1958
Komarovo

ПОСЛЕДНЯЯ

Услаждала бредами,
Пением могил.
Наделяла бедами
Свыше всяких сил.
Занавес неподнятый,
Хоровод теней, —
Оттого и отнятый
Был мне всех родней.
Это все поведано
Самой глуби роз.
Но забыть мне не дано
Вкус вчерашних слез.

1964

THE LAST ONE

I delighted in deliriums,
In singing about tombs.
I distributed misfortunes
Beyond anyone's strength.
The curtain not raised,
The circle dance of shades —
Because of that, all my loved ones
Were taken away.
All this is disclosed
In the depths of the roses.
But I am not allowed to forget
The taste of the tears of yesterday.

1964

РОДНАЯ ЗЕМЛЯ

И в мире нет людей бесслезней,
Надменнее и проще нас.
1922

В заветных ладанках не носим на груди,
О ней стихи навзрыд не сочиняем,
Наш горький сон она не бередит,
Не кажется обетованным раем,
Не делаем ее в душе своей
Предметом купли и продажи,
Хворая, бедствуя, немотствуя на ней,
О ней не вспоминаем даже.
Да, для нас это грязь на калошах,
Да, для нас это хруст на зубах.
И мы мелем, и месим, и крошим
Тот ни в чем не замешанный прах.
Но ложимся в нее и становимся ею,
Оттого и зовем так свободно — своею.

1961
Ленинград
Больница в Гавани

NATIVE LAND

But there is no people on earth more tearless,
More simple and more full of pride.
1922

We don't wear her on our breast in cherished amulets,
We don't, with wrenching sobs, write verse about her,
She does not disturb our bitter sleep,
Nor seem to us the promised paradise.
We have not made her, in our souls,
An object to be bought or sold.
Suffering, sick, wandering over her,
We don't even remember her.
  Yes, for us it's the mud on galoshes,
  Yes, for us it's the grit on our teeth.
  And we grind, and we knead, and we crumble
  This clean dust.
But we lie in her and we become her,
And because of that we freely call her — ours.

1961
Leningrad
The hospital in the harbor

ПОСЛЕДНЯЯ РОЗА

Вы напишеге о нас наискосок
И. Бродский

Мне с Морозовою класть поклоны,
С падчерицей Ирода плясать,
С дымом улетать с костра Дионы,
Чтобы с Жанной на костер опять.

Господи! Ты видишь, я устала
Воскресать, и умирать, и жить.
Все возьми, но этой розы алой
Дай мне свежесть снова ощутить.

9 августа 1962
Комарово

THE LAST ROSE

You will write about us on a slant.
J. Brodsky

I have to bow with Morozova,
Dance with Herod's stepdaughter,
fly up with the smoke of Dido's fire,
Only to return on Joan of Arc's pyre.

Lord! You see I am tired
Of living and dying and resurrection.
Take everything, but grant that I may feel
The freshness of this crimson rose again.

August 9, 1962
Komarovo

ПАМЯТИ В. С. СРЕЗНЕВСКОЙ

Почти не может быть, ведь ты была всегда:
В тени блаженных лип, в блокаде и в больнице,
В тюремной камере и там, где злые птицы,
И травы пышные, и страшная вода.
О, как менялось все, но ты была всегда,
И мнится, что души отъяли половину,
Ту, что была тобой, — в ней знала я причину
Чего-то главного. И всё забыла вдруг...
Но звонкий голос твой зовет меня оттуда
И просит не грустить и смерти ждать, как чуда,
Ну что ж! попробую.

9 сентября 1964
Комарово

TO THE MEMORY OF V. S. SREZNEVSKAYA

It almost cannot be, because you always were:
In the shadow of the blessed linden, in the siege and in
the hospital,
In the prison cell and there, where there were evil birds
And splendid grasses and dreadful tides.
Oh, how everything changed, but you always were,
And it seems as if they cut away half my soul,
The half that was you — and the main reason
For having it, I knew. And suddenly I forgot
everything …
But your ringing voice calls out to me from there,
And asks me not to grieve, but to wait for death as for a miracle.
All right! I'll try.

September 9, 1964
Komarovo

Северные Элегии

Все в жертву памяти твоей...
Пушкин

Первая

ПРЕДЫСТОРИЯ

Я теперь живу не там...
Пушкин

Россия Достоевского. Луна
Почти на четверть скрыта колокольней.
Торгуют кабаки, летят пролетки,
Пятиэтажные растут громады
В Гороховой, у Знаменья, под Смольным.
Везде танцклассы, вывески менял,
А рядом: «Henriette», «Basile», «André»
И пышные гроба: «Шумилов-старший».
Но, впрочем, город мало изменился.
Не я одна, но и другие тоже
Заметили, что он подчас умеет
Казаться литографией старинной,
Не первоклассной, но вполне пристойной,
Семидесятых, кажется, годов.
Особенно зимой, перед рассветом
Иль в сумерки — тогда за воротами
Темнеет жесткий и прямой Литейный,
Еще не опозоренный модерном,
И визави меня живут — Некрасов
И Салтыков...Обоим по доске
Мемориальной. О, как было б страшно
Им видеть эти доски! Прохожу.

Northern Elegies

Everything is a sacrifice to your memory ...
Pushkin

First

PREHISTORY

I no longer live there ...
Pushkin

Dostoevsky's Russia. The moon,
Almost a quarter hidden by the bell tower.
Pubs are bustling, droshkies flying,
In Gorokhovaya, near Znameniya and Smolny,
Huge, five-storied monstrosities are growing.
Dance classes everywhere, money changers' signs,
A line of shops: "Henriette," "Basile," "André"
And magnificent coffins: "Shumilov Senior."
But still, the city hasn't changed much.
Not only I, but others as well,
Have noticed that sometimes it could
Resemble an old lithograph,
Not first class, but fairly decent,
From the Seventies, I'd guess.
Especially in winter, before dawn,
Or at twilight — then behind the gates
Liteiny Boulevard darkens, rigid, straight,
Not yet disgraced by the Moderne,
And opposite me live — Nekrasov
And Saltikov ... Each on his memorial plaque.
Oh, how horrified they would be
To see those plaques! I move on.

А в Старой Руссе пышные канавы,
И в садиках подгнившие беседки,
И стекла окон так черны, как прорубь,
И мнится, там такое приключилось,
Что лучше не заглядывать, уйдем.
Не с каждым местом сговориться можно,
Чтобы оно свою открыло тайну
(А в Оптиной мне больше не бывать...).

Шуршанье юбок, клетчатые пледы,
Ореховые рамы у зеркал,
Каренинской красою изумленных,
И в коридорах узких те обои,
Которыми мы любовались в детстве,
Под желтой керосиновою лампой,
И тот же плюш на креслах...
                    Все разночинно, наспех, как-нибудь...
                    Отцы и деды непонятны Земли
                    Заложены. И в Бадене — рулетка.

И женщина с прозрачными глазами
(Такой глубокой синевы, что море
Нельзя не вспомнить, поглядевши в них),
С редчайшим именем и белой ручкой,
И добротой, которую в наследство
Я от нее как будто получила, —
Ненужный дар моей жестокой жизни...

Страну знобит, а омский каторжанин
Всё понял и на всем поставил крест.
Вот он сейчас перемешает всё
И сам над первозданным беспорядком,
Как некий дух, взнесется. Полночь бьет.
Перо скрипит, и многие страницы
Семеновским припахивают плацем.

And the splendid ditches of old Russa,
And the rotting arbors in the little gardens,
And a windowpane as black as a hole in the ice,
And it seems that such things happened here
That we'd better not look in. Let's leave.
Not every place agrees
To render up its secrets
(And I won't be in Optina anymore ...)

The rustle of skirts, the pattern of plaids,
The walnut frames of the mirrors
Amazed by Karenina's beauty,
And in the narrow hall the wallpaper
We feasted our eyes on in our childhood
By the yellow light of the kerosene lamp,
And the same plush on the armchairs ...
    Everything out of order, rushed, somehow ...
    Fathers and grandfathers incomprehensible.
    Lands mortgaged. And in Baden — roulette.

And a woman with translucent eyes
(Of such deep blue that to gaze into them
And not think of the sea was impossible),
With the rarest of names and white hands,
And a kindness that as an inheritance
I have from her, it seems —
Useless gift for my harsh life ...

The country shivers, and the convict from Omsk
Understood everything and made the sign of the cross over it all.
Now he shuffles everything around
And, over this primordial chaos,
Like some kind of spirit, he rises. Midnight sounds.
His pen squeaks, and page after page
Stinks of Semyonov Square.

Так вот когда мы вздумали родиться
И, безошибочно отмерив время,
Чтоб ничего не пропустить из зрелищ
Невиданных, простились с небытьем.

3 сентября 1940
Ленинград
Октябрь 1943
Ташкент

Вторая

Так вот он — тот осенний пейзаж,
Которого я так всю жизнь боялась:
И небо — как пылающая бездна,
И звуки города — как с того света
Услышанные, чуждые навеки,
Как будто все, с чем я внутри себя
Всю жизнь боролась, получило жизнь
Отдельную и воплотились в эти
Слепые стены, в этот черный сад...
А в ту минуту за плечом моим
Мой бывший дом еще следил за мною
Прищуренным, неблагосклонным оком,
Тем навсегда мне памятным окном.
Пятнадцать лет — пятнадцатью веками
Гранитными как будто притворились,
Но и сама была я как гранит:
Теперь моли, терзайся, называй
Морской царевной. Всё равно. Не надо...
Но надо было мне себя уверить,
Что это все случалось много раз,
И не со мной одной — с другими тоже,

This is when we decided to be born,
And timing it perfectly
So as not to miss any of those pageants
Yet to come, we bid farewell to non-existence.

September 3, 1940
Leningrad
October 1943
Tashkent

Second

So here it is — that autumn landscape
Of which I've been so frightened all my life:
And the sky — like a flaming abyss
And the sounds of the city — heard as if
From another world, forever strange:
It's as if everything I've struggled with inside myself
All my life received its own life
And bodied forth in these
Blind walls, in this black garden …
And right now, over my shoulder,
My old house still spies on me
With its squinting, disapproving eye,
That omnipresent window.
Fifteen years — pretending to be
Fifteen granite centuries,
But I myself was like granite:
Now beg, suffer, summon
The queen of the sea. It doesn't matter. No need to …
But I should have convinced myself
That all this has happened many times,
And not to me alone — to others too,

И даже хуже. Нет, не хуже — лучше.
И голос мой — и это, верно, было
Всего страшней — сказал из темноти:
«Пятнадцать лет назад какой ты песней
Встречала этот день, ты небеса,
И хоры звезд, и хоры вод молила
Приветствовать торжественную встречу
С тем, от кого сегодня ты ушла...

Так вот твоя серебряная свадьба:
Зови ж гостей, красуйся, торжествуй!»

Март 1942, Ташкент

Третая

Блажен, кто посетил сей мир
В его минуты роковые.
Тютчев

Н.А.О.

Меня, как реку,
Суровая эпоха повернула.
Мне подменили жизнь. В другое русло,
Мимо другого потекла она,
И я своих не знаю берегов.
О, как я много зрелищ пропустила,
И занавес вздымался без меня
И так же падал. Сколько я друзей
Своих ни разу в жизни не встречала,
И сколько очертаний городов
Из глаз моих могли бы вызвать слезы,

And even worse. No, not worse — better.
And my voice — and this, really,
Was the most frightening — uttered from the darkness:
"Fifteen years ago, with what rejoicing
You greeted this day, you begged the heavens
And the choirs of stars and the choirs of oceans
To salute the glorious meeting
With the one you left today …

So this is your silver anniversary:
Summon the guests, stand in splendor, celebrate!"

March 1942, Tashkent

Third

Blessed is he who visits this world
At his appointed hour.
Tyutchev

N. A. O.

I, like a river,
Was rechanneled by this stern age.
They gave me a substitute life. It began to flow
In a different course, passing the other one,
And I do not recognize my banks.
Oh, how many spectacles I've missed,
And the curtain rose without me
And then fell. How many of my friends
I've never met once in my life,
And how many cities' skylines
Could have drawn tears from my eyes;

А я один на свете город знаю
И ощупью его во сне найду.
И сколько я стихов не написала,
И тайный хор их бродит вкруг меня
И, может быть, еще когда-нибудь
Меня задушит...
Мне ведомы начала и концы,
И жизнь после конца, и что-то,
О чем теперь не надо вспоминать.
И женщина какая-то мое
Единственное место заняла,
Мое законнейшее имя носит,
Оставивши мне кличку, из которой
Я сделала, пожалуй, все, что можно.
Я не в свою, увы, могилу лягу.
Но иногда весенний шалый ветер,
Иль сочетанье слов в случайной книге,
Или улыбка чья-то вдруг потянут
Меня в несостоявшуюся жизнь.
В таком году произошло бы то-то,
А в этом — это: ездить, видеть, думать,
И вспоминать, и в новую любовь
Входить, как в зеркало, с тупым сознаньем
Измены и с еще вчера не бывшей
Морщинкой.
. . . .
Но если бы оттуда посмотрела
Я на свою теперешнюю жизнь,
Узнала бы я зависть наконец...

2 сентября 1945
Ленинград

But I only know one city in the world
And I could find my way around it in my sleep.
And how many poems I didn't write,
And their mysterious chorus prowls around me,
And, perhaps, may yet somehow
Strangle me …
I am aware of beginnings and endings,
And life after the end, and something
That I don't have to remember just now.
And some other woman occupied
The special place reserved for me
And bears my legal name,
Leaving me the nickname, with which
I did, probably, everything that could be done.
I will not lie down, alas, in my own grave.
But sometimes the playful spring wind
Or the combination of words in some book,
Or somebody's smile suddenly drags
Me into that life that never took place.
In this year, such and such would have happened,
In that year — that: traveling, seeing, thinking
And remembering, and entering into a new love
As into a mirror, with dim awareness
Of betrayal and of the wrinkle
That wasn't there the day before.

. . . .

But had I observed from there
The life I am living today,
I would finally discover envy …

September 2, 1945
Leningrad

Четвертая

Последний ключ — холодный ключ забвенья.
Он слаще всех жар сердца утолит.

Пушкин

Есть три эпохи у воспоминаний.
И первая — как бы вчерашний день.
Душа под сводом их благословенным,
И тело в их блаженствует тени.
Еще не замер смех, струятся слезы,
Пятно чернил не стерто со стола, —
И как печать на сердце, поцелуй,
Единственный, прощальный, незабвенный...
Но это продолжается недолго...
Уже не свод над головой, а где-то
В глухом предместье дом уединенный,
Где холодно зимой, а летом жарко,
Где есть паук и пыль на всем лежит,
Где истлевают пламенные письма,
Исподтишка меняются портреты,
Куда как на могилу ходят люди,
А возвратившись, моют руки мылом,
И стряхивают беглую слезнику
С усталых век — и тяжело вздыхают...
Но тикают часы, весна сменяет
Одна другую, розовеет небо,
Меняются названья городов,
И нет уже свидетелей событий,
И не с кем плакать, не с кем вспоминать.
И медленно от нас уходят тени,
Которых мы уже не призываем,
Возврат которых был бы страшен нам.
И, раз проснувшись, видим, что забыли
Мы даже путь в тот дом уединенный,

Fourth

The last key — is the cold key of oblivion.
It gives sweeter satisfaction than all the ardors of the heart.
Pushkin

There are three ages to memories,
And the first — is like just yesterday.
The soul is under their blissful arch,
And the body basks in their blissful shade.
Laughter has not yet died, tears flow,
The ink blot on the desk has not faded —
And, like a seal on the heart, the kiss,
Unique, valedictory, unforgettable …
But this does not long endure …
Already there is no arch overhead, but somewhere
In a remote suburb, a solitary house,
Where it is cold in winter, hot in summer,
Where there are spiders, and dust on everything,
Where ardent letters are decomposing,
Portraits are stealthily changing.
People walk to this house as if to their grave,
And wash their hands with soap when they return,
And blink away a facile tear
From weary eyes — and breathe out heavy sighs …
But the clock ticks, one springtime is superseded
By another, the sky glows pink,
Names of cities change
And there are no remaining witnesses to the events,
And no one to weep with, no one to remember with.
And slowly the shades withdraw from us,
Shades we no longer call back,
Whose return would be too terrible for us.
And waking one morning we realize that we have forgotten
Even the path to that solitary house,

И, задыхаясь от стыда и гнева,
Бежим туда, но (как во сне бывает)
Там всё другое: люди, вещи, стены,
И нас никто не знает — мы чужие.
Мы не туда попали...Боже мой!
И вот когда горчайшее приходит:
Мы сознаем, что не могли б вместить
То прошлое в границы нашей жизни,
И нам оно почти что так же чуждо,
Как нашему соседу по квартире,
Что тех, кто умер, мы бы не узнали,
А те, с кем нам разлуку бог послал,
Прекрасно обошлись без нас — и даже
Всё к лучшему...

5 февраля 1945
Ленинград

Пятая

О ДЕСЯТЫХ ГОДАХ

Ты — победительница жизни,
И я — товарищ вольный твой.
Н. Гумилев

И никакого розового детства . . .
Веснушечек, и мишек, и кудряшек,
И добрых теть, и страшных дядь, и даже
Приятелей средь камешков речных.
Себе самой я с самого начала
То чьим-то сном казалась или бредом,
Иль отраженьем в зеркале чужом,

And, choking with anger and shame,
We run there, but (as it happens in dreams),
Everything has changed: the people, the objects, the walls,
And nobody knows us — we are strangers.
We don't find ourselves there ... My God!
And then it is that bitterness wells up:
We realize that we couldn't have fit
That past into the boundaries of our life,
And that it is almost as foreign to us
As to our next-door neighbor,
That those who died we wouldn't recognize,
And those from whom God separated us
Got along perfectly well without us — and even
That everything turned out for the best ...

February 5, 1945
Leningrad

Fifth

ABOUT THE 1910'S

You — the conqueror of life,
And I — your unfettered friend.
N. Gumilyov

And there was no rosy childhood ...
Freckles and toy bears and curls,
And doting aunts and scary uncles, or even
Friends among the river pebbles.
I myself, from the very beginning,
Seemed to myself like someone's dream or delirium,
Or a reflection in someone else's mirror,

Без имени, без плоти, без причины.
Уже я знала список преступлений,
Которые должна я совершить.
И вот я, лунатически ступая,
Вступила в жизнь и испугала жизнь:
Она передо мною сталась лугом,
Где некогда гуляла Прозерпина,
Передо мнлй, безродной, неумелой,
Открылись неожиданные двери,
И выходили люди, и кричали:
«Она пришла, она пришла сама!»
А я на них глядела с изумленьем
И думала: «Они с ума сошли!»
И чем сильней они меня хвалили,
Чем мной сильнее люди восхищались,
Тем мне страшнее было в мире жить
И тем сильней хотелось пробудиться,
И знала я, что заплачу сторицей
В тюрьме, в могиле, в сумасшедшем доме,
Везде, где просыпаться надлежит
Таким, как я, — но длилась пытка счастьем.

4 июля 1955
Москва

Without flesh, without meaning, without a name.
Already I knew the list of crimes
That I was destined to commit.
And so, wandering like a somnambulist,
I stepped into life and startled it:
It stretched before me like the meadow
Where once Proserpina strolled.
Before me, who was without family, unskilled,
Doors unexpectedly opened
And people streamed out and exclaimed:
"She came, she herself came!"
But I looked at them in astonishment
And I thought: "They must be mad!"
And the more they praised me,
The more people admired me,
The more frightful it was to live in the world,
And the more I yearned to awaken,
For I knew that I would pay dearly
In prison, in the grave, in the madhouse,
Wherever someone like me must awaken —
But the torture dragged on as good fortune.

July 4, 1955
Moscow

Шестая

В том доме было очень страшно жить,
И ни камина свет патриархальный,
Ни колыбелька моего ребенка,
Ни то, что оба молоды мы были
И замыслов исполнены,
[. . . . . и удача
От нашего порога ни на шаг
За все семь лет не смела отойти, —]
Не уменьшало это чувство страха.
И я над ним смеяться научилась
И оставляла капельку вина
И крошки хлеба для того, кто ночью
Собакою царапался у двери
Иль в низкое заглядывал окошко,
В то время, как мы, замолчав, старались
Не видеть, что творится в зазеркалье,
Под чьими тяжеленными шагами
Стонали темной лестницы ступени,
Как о пощаде жалостно моля,
И говорил ты, странно улыбаясь:
«Кого *они* по лестнице несут?»

Теперь ты там, где знают все, — скажи:
Что в этом доме жило кроме нас?

1921
Царское Село

Sixth

It was dreadful to live in that house,
And not the patriarchal glow of the hearth,
Not the cradle of my child,
Not the fact that we were both young
And full of ideas,
. . . . . and that good fortune
Didn't dare take a step from our door
For seven years,
Nothing diminished that feeling of fear.
And I learned to laugh at it,
And I left a drop of wine
And crumbs of bread for the one who every night
Scratched like a dog at the door
Or peered through the low-set window,
While we, keeping still, tried
Not to see what was happening behind the mirror,
Under whose heavy tread
The steps of the dark staircase groaned,
As if pleading dolefully for mercy,
And you said, smiling strangely:
"Who are *they* dragging down the stairs?"

Now that you're there, where everything is known — tell me:
What else lived in that house besides us?

1921
Tsarskoe Selo

Седьмая

А я молчу, я тридцать лет молчу.
Молчание арктическими льдами
Стоит вокруг бессчетными ночами,
Оно идет гасить мою свечу.
Так мертвые молчат, но то понятно
И менее ужесно. . . . .

Мое молчанье слышится повсюду,
Оно судебный наполняет зал,
И самый гул молвы перекричать
Оно могло бы, и подобно чуду
Оно на все кладет свою печать.
Оно во всем участвует, о Боже!
Кто мог придумать мне такую рол?
Стать на кого-нибудь чуть-чуть похожей,
О Господи! — мне хоть на миг позволь.
. . . .
И разве я не выпила цикуту,
Так почему же я не умерла
Как следует — в ту самую минуту?
. . . .
Нет, не тому, кто ищет эти книги,
Кто их украл, кто даже переплел,
Кто носит их, как тайные вериги,
Кто наизусть запомнил каждый слог
. . . .
Нет, не к тому летит мое мечтанье,
И не тому отдам я благодать,
А лишь тому, кто смел мое молчанье
На стяге очевидном — написать,
И кто с ним жил, и кто в него поверил,
Кто бездну ту кромешную измерил
. . . .

Seventh

And I have been silent, silent for thirty years.
The silence of arctic ice
Stands through innumerable nights,
Closing in to snuff out my candle.
The dead are silent like this, but that's understandable
And not as horrible. . . . .

My silence can be heard everywhere.
It fills the courtroom,
And it could have drowned out
The roar of rumor, and like a miracle
It puts its stamp on everything.
It is part of everything. O God!
Who could have thought up such a role for me?
Allow me for a moment, O Lord,
To begin to become a little bit like someone else.

. . . .

And could it be I haven't drunk hemlock?
So why didn't I die
As I should have — then and there?

. . . .

No, not to the one who is searching for these books,
Who stole them, who even bound them,
Who carries them around like secret chains,
Who memorized every syllable

. . . .

No, not to that one does my dream fly,
And not to that one will I give my blessing,
But only to the one who dared
To hoist my silence on a banner,
Who lived with it, and who believed in it,
Who took the measure of this pitch-dark, bottomless pit

. . . .

Мое молчанье в музыке и песне
И в чьей-то омерзительной любви,
В разлуках, в книгах. . .
                        В том, что неизвестней
Всего на свете. . . . .
. . . .
Я и сама его подчас пугаюсь,
Когда оно всей тяжестью своей
Теснит меня, дыша и надвигаясь.
Защиты нет, нет ничего — скорей.
Кто знает, как оно окаменело,
Как выжгло сердце и каким огнем,
Подумаешь. Кому какое дело,
Всем так уютно и привычно в нем.
Его со мной делить согласны все вы,
Но все-таки оно всегда мое.
. . . .
Оно мою почти сожрало душу,
Оно мою уродует судьбу,
Но я его когда-нибудь нарушу,
Чтоб смерть позвать к позорному столбу.

1958-1964
Ленинград

My silence is in music and in song
And in somebody's loathsome love,
In parting, in books ...
                    In what is least known
In the world . . . .
. . . .
I myself am sometimes afraid of it,
When with all its weight
It presses on me, breathing and drawing close:
There is no defense, or rather — there is nothing.
Who knows how it turned to stone.
You can imagine how it scorched my heart
And with what kind of fire. Whose concern is it?
Everyone feels so comfortable and accustomed to it.
All of you agree to share it,
Nevertheless it is always mine
. . . .
It is deforming my fate,
It almost devoured my soul,
But I will break it some day
To summon death to the whipping post.

1958-1964
Leningrad

В углу старик, похожий на барана,
Внимательно читает «Фигаро».
В моей руке просохшее перо,
Идти домой еще как будто рано.

Тебе велела я, чтоб ты ушел.
Мне сразу всё твои глаза сказали...
Опилки густо устилают пол
И пахнет спиртом в полукруглой зале

И это юность — светлая пора
. . . .
Да лучше б я повесилась вчера
Или под поезд бросилась сегодня.

Весна 1911
Париж

In the corner an old man resembling a ram
Is poring over *Figaro*.
In my hand an idle pen,
It's still too early to go home.

I ordered you to leave.
Your eyes told me everything instantly …
The floor is thick in sawdust
And the half-moon hall smells of alcohol

And this is youth — that glorious time
. . . .
I should have hanged myself yesterday
Or thrown myself under a train today.

Spring 1911
Paris

Здесь беда со мной случилась,
Первая моя беда.
Из линючих туч сочилась
Леденистая вода.

День был скудный и жестокий,
Всех минувших дней бледней.
Где же были вы, упреки
Чуткой совести моей?

. . . .
. . . .
И себя я помню тонкой
Смуглой девочкой в чадре.
. . . .бубенчик звонкий,
Кони ждали на дворе.

Июнь 1914
Слепнево

Some great misfortune happened to me here,
My first misfortune.
Icy water oozed
From fading clouds.

The day was stingy and cruel,
Of all days the most pale,
And where were you,
My keen conscience's rebukes?

. . . .
. . . .
And I still remember myself as a dark,
Slender little girl in a veil.
. . . . bells tinkling,
Horses stood waiting in the courtyard.

June 1914
Slepnyovo

А. А. Блоку

Ты первый, ставший у источника
С улыбкой мертвой и сухой,
Как нас измучил взор пустой,
Твой взор тяжелый – полунощника.
Но годы страшные пройдут,
Ты скоро будешь снова молод,
И сохраним мы тайный холод
Тебе отсчитанных минут.

Между 1912 и 1914

— to Alexander Blok

You, the leader, standing by the spring
Smiling a dry, dead smile,
How the vacant stare tormented us,
Your haggard stare — a night owl.
But the terrible years will pass,
You will soon be young again,
And we will preserve the mysterious chill
Of the minutes we counted off for you then.

Between 1912 and 1914

БЕЛАЯ НОЧЬ

Небо бело страшной белизною,
А земля как уголь и гранит.
Под иссохшей этою луною
Ничего уже не заблестит.

Женский голос, хриплый и задорный,
Не поет, кричит, кричит.
Надо мною близко тополь черный
Ни одним листком не шелестит.

Для того ль тебя я целовала,
Для того ли мучилась, любя,
Чтоб теперь спокойно и устало
С отвращеньем вспоминать тебя?

17 июня 1914
Слепнево

WHITE NIGHT

A sky white with a frightful whiteness,
And the earth like coal and granite.
Under this withered moon
Nothing shines anymore.

A woman's voice, hoarse and impassioned,
Doesn't sing, but yells, yells.
On the black poplar right above me
Not a single leaf rustles.

Was this why I kissed you?
Was this why I tormented myself, loving?
To remember you now, calmly and wearily,
With loathing?

June 17, 1914
Slepnyovo

В городе райского ключаря,
В городе мертвого царя
Майские зори красны и желты,
Церкви белы, высоки мосты.
И в темном саду между старых лип
Мачт корабельных слышится скрип.
А за окошком моим река —
Никто не знает, как глубока.
Вольно я выбрала дивный Град,
Жаркое солнце земных отрад,
И все мне казалось, что в Раю
Я песню последнюю пою.

1917

In the city of the gatekeeper of paradise,
In the city of the dead tsar,
The May dawns are red and yellow,
The churches white, the bridges high.
And in the dark garden among the old lindens,
The creaking of ship masts is heard
And there is a river beyond my window —
How deep, nobody knows.
I chose this marvelous city of my own accord,
This burning heart of earthly delights,
And it always seemed to me that I was singing
My latest song in paradise.

1917

Так просто можно жизнь покинуть эту,
Бездумно и безбольно догореть,
Но не дано Российскому поэту
Такою светлой смертью умереть.

Всего верней свинец душе крылатой
Небесные откроет рубежи
Иль хриплый ужас лапою косматой
Из сердца, как из губки, выжмет жизнь.

1925

It would be so easy to abandon this life,
To burn down painlessly and unaware,
But it is not given to the Russian poet
To die a death so pure.

A bullet more reliably throws open
Heaven's boundaries to the soul in flight,
Or hoarse terror with a shaggy paw can,
As if from a sponge, squeeze out the heart's life.

1925

Зачем вы отравили воду
И с грязью мой смешали хлеб?
Зачем последнюю свободу
Вы превращаете в вертеп?
За то, что я не надругалась
Над горькой гибелью друзей,
За то, что я верна осталась
Печальной родине моей?
Пусть так. Без палача и плахи
Поэту на земле не быть.
Нам покаянные рубахи,
Нам со свечей идти и выть.

1935

Why did you poison the water
And mix dirt with my bread?
Why did you turn the last freedom
Into a den of thieves?
Because I didn't jeer
At the bitter death of friends?
Because I remained true
To my sorrowing motherland?
So be it. Without hangman and scaffold
A poet cannot exist in the world.
Our lot is to wear the hair shirt,
To walk with a candle and to wail.

1935

ПОДРАЖАНИЕ АРМЯНСКОМУ

Я приснюсь тебе черной овцою
На нетвердых, сухих ногах,
Подойду, заблею, завою:
«Сладко ль ужинал, падишах?
Ты вселенную держишь, как бусу,
Светлой волей Аллаха храним...
И пришелся ль сынок мой по вкусу
И тебе и деткам твоим?»

1930-е годы

IMITATION FROM THE ARMENIAN

I will appear in your dreams as a black ewe,
On withered, unsteady legs
I will approach you, begin to bleat, to howl:
"Padishah, have you supped daintily?
You hold the universe, like a bead,
You are cherished by Allah's radiant will ...
And was he tasty, my little son?
Did he please you, please your children?"

1930's

ПАМЯТИ М. Б-ВА

Вот это я тебе, взамен могильных роз,
Взамен кадильного куренья;
Ты так сурово жил и до конца донес
Великолепное презренье.
Ты пил вино, ты как никто шутил
И в душных стенах задыхался,
И гостью страшную ты сам к себе впустил,
И с ней наедине остался.
И нет тебя, и всё вокруг молчит
О скорбной и высокой жизни,
Лишь голос мой, как флейта, прозвучит
И на твоей безмольвной тризне.
О, кто поверить смел, что полоумной мне,
Мне, плакальщице дней погибших,
Мне, тлеющей на медленном огне,
Все потерявшей, всех забывшей, —
Придется поминать того, кто, полный сил,
И светлых замыслов, и воли,
Как будто бы вчера со мною говорил,
Скрывая дрожь предсмертной боли.

Март 1940
Фонтанный Дом

TO THE MEMORY OF M. B.

I give you this instead of roses on your grave,
Instead of the burning of incense;
You lived so sparely and, to the end, maintained
That magnificent disdain.
You drank wine, you joked like nobody else
And suffocated between those stifling walls,
And you yourself let in the terrible guest
And stayed with her alone.
And you are no more, and nothing is heard anywhere
About your noble and sorrowful life,
Only my voice, like a flute, sounds
At your silent funeral service.
Oh, who dared believe that I, half mad,
I, the mourner of perished days,
I, smoldering over a low flame,
Having lost everything and forgotten everyone —
I would have to commemorate the one who, full of strength,
And will, and brilliant schemes,
Talked to me just yesterday it seems,
Concealing the trembling of mortal pain.

March 1940
Fountain House

ПОЗДНИЙ ОТВЕТ

Белорученька моя, чернокнижница.
М. Ц.

Невидимка, двойник, пересмешник,
Что ты прячешься в черных кустах,
То забьешься в дырявый скворешник,
То мелькнешь на погибших крестах.
То кричишь из Маринкиной башни:
«Я сегодня вернулась домой,
Полюбуйтесь, родимые пашни,
Что за это случилось со мной.
Поглотила любимых пучина,
И разграблен родительский дом».
Мы сегодня с тобою, Марина,
По столице полночной идем,
А за нами таких миллионы,
И безмолвнее шествия нет,
А вокруг погребальные звоны
Да московские дикие стоны
Вьюги, наш заметающей след.

16 марта 1940
Фонтанный Дом – Красная Конница

BELATED REPLY

My white-handed one, dark princess.
M.Ts.

Invisible, double, jester,
You who are hiding in the depths of the bushes,
The one crouching in a starling house,
The one flitting on the crosses of the dead.
The one crying from the Marinkina Tower:
"I have come home today.
Native fields, cherish me
Because of what happened to me.
The abyss swallowed my loved ones,
The family home has been plundered."
We are together today, Marina,
Walking through the midnight capital,
And behind us there are millions like us,
And never was a procession more hushed,
Accompanied by funeral bells
And the wild, Moscow moans
Of a snowstorm erasing all traces of us.

Fountain House
Krasnaya Konitsa
March 16, 1940

De profundis...Мое поколенье
Мало меду вкусило. И вот
Только ветер гудит в отдаленьи,
Только память о мертвых поет.
Наше было не кончено дело,
Наши были часы сочтены,
До желанного водораздела,
До вершины великой горы,
До неистового цветенья
Оставалось лишь раз вздохнуть...
Две войны, мое поколенье,
Освещали твой страшный путь.

23 марта 1944
Ташкент

De profundis … My generation
Tasted little honey. And now
Only the wind hums in the distance,
Only memory sings about the dead.
Our work was not finished,
Our hours were numbered,
Till of that long-awaited watershed,
Till of that great mountain's peak,
Till of that violent flowering
Remained only one breath …
Two wars, my generation,
Lit your terrible path.

March 23, 1944
Tashkent

Ин. Басалаеву на память о нашем Ташкенте

Не знала б, как цветет айва,
Не знала б, как звучат слова
На вашем языке,
Как в город с гор ползет туман,
И что проходит караван
Чрез пыльный Бешагач
Как луч, как ветер, как поток...

*

И город древен, как земля,
Из чистой глины сбитый.
Вокруг бескрайние поля
Тюльпанами залиты.

*

Теперь я всех благодарю,
Рахмат и хайер говорю
И вам машу платком.
Рахмат, Айбек, рахмат, Чусти,
Рахмат, Тошкент! — прости, прости,
Мой тихий древний дом.
Рахмат и звездам, и цветам,
И маленьким баранчукам
У чернокосых матерей
На молодых руках...
Я восемьсот волшебных дней
Под ситней чашею твоей,
Лапислазурной чашей
Тобой дышала, жгучий сад...

28 сентября 1945
Ленинград

— to I. M. Basalaev in memory of our Tashkent

I wouldn't have known how the quince tree blossoms,
I wouldn't have known how words sound
In your tongue,
How the fog crawls down the mountain to the city,
And that a caravan is crossing
Dusty Beshagach
Like the wind, like a stream, like a ray …

*

And the city is ancient, like the earth,
Beaten out of pure clay
And surrounded by boundless fields,
floods of tulips.

*

Now I thank everyone,
Rakhmat and *khaier* I say,
Waving my scarf.
Rakhmat, Aibek, *rakhmat*, Chusti,
Rakhmat, Toshkent! Goodbye, goodbye,
My quiet, ancient home.
Rakhmat also the flowers and to the stars,
And to the little *baranchuks*
In the youthful arms
Of mothers with black braids …
I was eight hundred magical days
Under your deep blue cup,
Lapis lazuli cup
I breathed you, garden aflame …

September 28, 1945
Leningrad

...Да пустыни немых площадей,
Где казнили людей до рассвета.
Инн. Анненский

Все ушли и никто не вернулся.
Только верный обету любви,
Мой последний, лишь ты оглянулся,
Чтоб увидеть все небо в крови.
Дом был проклят, и проклято дело.
Тщетно песня звенела нежней,
И глаза я поднять не посмела
Перед страшной судьбою своей.
Осквернили пречистое Слово,
Растоптали священный глагол,
Чтоб с сиделками тридцать седьмого
Мыла я окровавленный пол.
Разлучили с единственным сыном,
В казематах пытали друзей,
Окружили невидимым тыном
Крепко слаженной слежки своей.
Наградили меня немотою,
На весь мир окаянно кляня,
Обкормили меня клеветою,
Опоили отравой меня.
И до самого края доведши,
Почему-то оставили там —
Буду я городской сумасшедшей
По притихшим бродить пдощадям.

Конец 40-х гг.

. . . And the deserts of mute squares,
Where people were executed before dawn.
I. Annensky

Everyone left and no one returned,
Only, true to the promise of love,
My latest, at least you looked back
To see the whole sky in blood.
The house was cursed, and cursed was my trade;
Uselessly, a tender song rang out
And I didn't dare raise my eyes
To my terrible fate.
They defiled the immaculate Word,
They trampled the sacred utterance,
So that with the sicknurses of Thirty-Seven
I could mop the bloody floor.
They separated me from my only son,
They tortured my friends in prisons,
They surrounded me with an invisible stockade
Of well coordinated shadowing.
They rewarded me with a muteness
That curses the whole cursed world,
They force-fed me with scandal,
They made me drink poison.
And taking me to the very edge,
For some reason they left me there.
I would rather, as one of the city's "crazies,"
Be wandering through the dying squares.

End of the 40's

ЗАСТОЛЬНАЯ

Под узорной скатертью
Не видать стола.
Я стихам не матерью —
Мачехой была.
Эх, бумага белая,
Строчек ровный ряд!
Сколько раз глядела я,
Как они горят.
Сплетней изувечены,
Биты кистенем,
Мечены, мечены
Каторжным клеймом.

1955

FESTIVE SONG

Under the embroidered tablecloth,
        No table to be seen.
I was not mother to the poems —
        But stepmother.
Ach! White paper,
        Straight row of lines!
How many times I've watched
        Them burn.
Maimed by gossip,
        Beaten with bludgeons,
Stamped, stamped
        With the convict's brand.

1955

Другие уводят любимых, —
Я с зависитью вслед не гляжу,
Одна на скамье подсудимых
Я скоро полвека сижу.
Вокруг словоблудье и давка
И приторный запах чернил.
Такое выдумывал Кафка
И Чарли изобразил.
И так в пререканиях важных,
Как в цепких объятиях сна,
Все три поколенья присяжных
Решили: «виновна она».
Меняются лица конвоя,
В инфаркте шестой прокурор...
А где-то чернеет от зноя
Огромный небесный простор,
И полное прелести лето
Гуляет на том берегу...
Я это блаженное «где-то»
Представить себе не могу.
Я глохну от зычных проклятий,
Я ватник сносила дотла...
Неужто я всех виноватей
На этой планете была?

(Середина 50-х гг.)

Others go off with their loved ones —
I don't look after them with envy.
I've been sitting alone in the prisoner's dock
For almost half a century,
Surrounded by quarrels and crowds
And the cloying smell of ink.
It's like something invented by Kafka
And played by Chaplin.
And in these momentous arguments,
As in the tenacious embrace of sleep,
Three generations of juries
Decided: "She is guilty."
The faces of the guards change,
The sixth procurator has a heart attack …
And somewhere heaven's huge space
Darkens with heat,
And a whole summer of loveliness
Strolls on that shore …
I can't even imagine
That blessed "somewhere" anymore.
I've been deafened by shouted curses,
I've worn out my prisoner's jacket.
Am I really more guilty than anyone
Who ever lived on this planet?

Middle of the 50's

Забудут? — вот чéм удивили!
Меня забывали сто раз,
Стог раз я лежала в могиле,
Где, может быть, я и сейчас.
А Муза и глохла и слепла,
В земле истлевала зерном,
Чтоб после, как Феникс из пепла,
В эфире восстать голубом.

21 февраля 1957
Ленинград

They will forget? — How astonishing!
They forgot me a hundred times,
A hundred times I lay in the grave,
Where, perhaps, I am today.
But the Muse, both deaf and blind,
Rotted in the ground, like grain,
Only, like the Phoenix from the ashes,
To rise into the blue ether again.

February 21, 1957
Leningrad

И меня по ошибке пленило,
Как нарядная пляшет беда . . .
Все тогда по-тогдашнему было,
По-тогдашнему было тогда.
. . . .
Я спала в королевской кровати,
Голодала, носила дрова,
Там еще от похвал и проклятий
Не кружилась моя голова...

13 августа 1960

I was captivated by mistake,
Misfortune danced like an elegant woman …
At that time that's how it was,
That's how it was at that time.

. . . .

I slept in the king's bed,
Hungry, I carried wood,
Then neither praises nor curses
Had yet turned my head …

August 13, 1960

ТВОРЧЕСТВО

…говорит оно:
Я помню все в одно и то же время,
Вселенную перед собой, как бремя
Нетрудное в протянутой руке,
Как дальний свет на дальнем маяке,
Несу, а в недрах тайно зреет семя
Грядущего…

14 ноября 1959
Ленинград

CREATION

… it says:
I remember everything simultaneously;
Like the distant beam of a distant lighthouse,
I carry the universe before me
Like an easy burden in an outstretched palm,
And in the depths, mysteriously growing, is the seed
Of what is to come …

November 14, 1959
Leningrad

Вам жить, а мне не очень,
Тот близок поворот.
О, как он строг и точен,
Незримого расчет.

Зверей стреляют разно,
Есть каждому черед
Весьма разнообразный,
Но волка — круглый год.

Волк любит жить на воле,
Но с волком скор расчет:
На льду, в лесу и в поле
Бьют волка круглый год.

Не плачь, о друг единый,
Коль летом иль зимой
Опять с тропы волчиной
Услышишь голос мой.

1959

You are to live, but I, not very much longer,
The turning point is close at hand.
Oh, how strict it is, how exacting,
The invisible accounting.

They hunt beasts in different ways,
Each one's turn
Quite different,
But the wolf — the year round.

The wolf loves to live in freedom,
But the wolf is soon brought to account:
On the ice, in the forest, in the fields,
They slaughter the wolf all year long.

Oh, don't weep, my only friend,
If from the wolf path
In summer or in winter
You hear my voice again.

1959

Хвалы эти мне не по чину,
И Сафо совсем ни при чем,
Я знаю другую причину,
О ней мы с тобой не прочтем.
Пусть кто-то спасается бегством,
Другие кивают из ниш,
Стихи эти были с подтекстом
Таким, что как в бездну глядишь.
А бездна та манит и тянет,
И ввек не доищешься дна,
И ввек говорить не устанет
Пустая ее тишина.

(1959)

These praises for me are not due to rank,
And Sappho has nothing to do with it.
I know another reason,
But we won't read about it.
Let whoever wants to escape by flight,
Others nod from a niche.
These poems have such hidden meanings
It's like staring into an abyss.
And the abyss is enticing and beckoning,
And never will you discover the bottom of it,
And never will its hollow silence
Grow tired of speaking.

(1959)

СЛУШАЯ ПЕНИЕ

Женский голос как ветер несется,
Черным кажется, влажным, ночным,
И чего на лету ни коснется —
Все становится сразу иным.
Заливает алмазным сияньем,
Где-то что-то на миг серебрит
И загадочным одеяньем
Небывалых шелков шелестит.
И такая могучая сила
Зачарованный голос влечет,
Будто там впереди не могила,
А таинственной лестницы взлет.

19 декабря 1961 (Никола Зимний)
Больница им. Ленина
(Вишневская пела «Бразильскую баховиану»)

LISTENING TO SINGING

A woman's voice is rushing like the wind,
Black, it seems, damp, and of the night.
And whatever it touches in its flight —
Becomes instantly transformed.
With a diamond shining it pours,
Somewhere, something silvers for a moment
And an intriguing garment
Of fabulous silks rustles.
And such a compelling power
Draws the bewitched voice on,
As if ahead there were no grave,
But the flight of a flight of mysterious stairs.

December 19, 1961 (St. Nicholas Day)
Lenin Hospital
(Vishnevskaya sings the Bachianas Brasileiras*)*

ВЫХОД КНИГИ
(Из цикла «Тайны ремесла»)

Тот день всегда необычаен.
Скрывая скуку, горечь, злость,
Поэт — приветливый хозяин,
Читатель — благосклонный гость.

Один ведет гостей в хоромы,
Другой — под своды шалаша,
А третий — прямо в ночь истомы,
Моим — и дыба хороша.

Зачем, какие и откуда
И по дороге в никуда,
Что их влечет — какое чудо,
Какая черная звезда?

Но всем им несомненно ясно,
Каких за это ждать наград,
Что оставаться здесь опасно,
Что это не Эдемский сад.

А вот поди ж! Опять нахлынут,
И этот час неотвратим...
И мимоходом сердце вынут
Глухим сочувствием своим.

13 августа 1962 (днем)
Комарово

THE PUBLICATION OF A BOOK
(From the Cycle "Secrets of the Craft")

That day is always unusual.
Concealing boredom, bitterness and malice,
The poet is — a friendly host,
The reader — an appreciative guest.

One leads the guests into a mansion,
Another — under the pitched roof of a hut,
A third — directly into a night of languor,
For my readers — the rack is good enough.

Why, what sort are they and from where,
And along this road to nowhere,
What lures them — what miracle,
What black star?

But to all of them it's unquestionably clear
What kind of reward to expect,
That it is dangerous to stay here,
That this is not the Garden of Eden.

But just imagine! They keep surging in,
Inevitably …
And, in passing, they bear my heart away
With their deaf sympathy.

August 13, 1962 (afternoon)
Komarovo

СЕВЕР

Запад клеветал и сам же верил
И роскошно предавал Восток;
Юг мне воздух очень скупо мерил,
Ухмыляясь из-за бойких строк.
Но стоял, как на коленях, клевер;
Влажный месяц пел в жемчужный рог,
Так мой старый друг, мой верный Север
Утешал меня, как только мог.
В душной изнывала я истоме,
Задыхалась в смраде и крови,
Не могла я больше в этом доме...
Вот когда железная Суоми
Молвила: «Ты все узнаешь, кроме
Радости. А ничего, живи!»

1964

THE NORTH

The West slandered and believed itself,
And the East luxuriously betrayed,
The South doled out air for me stingily,
Grinning from behind clever lines.
But the clover stood as if on its knees,
The damp wind blew into a horn of pearl,
Thus my old friend, my true North,
Comforted me as well as it could.
I languished in stifling lassitude,
I suffocated in stench and blood,
I couldn't bear this house any more …
That's when iron Finland
Declared: "You will know everything, except
Joy. Even so, live!"

1964

В СОЧЕЛЬНИК (24 ДЕКАБРЯ)
Последний день в Риме

Заключенье небывшего цикла
Часто сердцу труднее всего,
Я от многого в жизни отвыкла,
Мне не нужно почти ничего, —

Для меня комаровские сосны
На своих языках говорят
И совсем как отдельные весны
В лужах, выпивших небо, — стоят.

1964

CHRISTMASTIME (DECEMBER 24)
Last Day in Rome

The conclusion of an imaginary cycle
Is often harder for the heart to bear,
I gave up many things in life,
There is almost nothing that I need any more —

For me, Komarovo's pines
Speak a language all their own,
And like entirely separate springtimes
They stand, each in a pool that has drunk up the sky.

1964

Notes to Poems

p. 29

Tsarskoye Selo — literally, "the tsar's village," is near Petersburg. Akhmatova grew up there. It is a town with huge parks and allées of splendid lindens. The imperial summer residence, Catherine's Palace, was located there and the lycée adjacent to the palace was attended by Pushkin.

p. 31

Line 1 — The "dark-skinned youth" is Pushkin, whose ancestry included Prince Hannibal of Abyssinia, an African and protégé of Peter the Great.

Line 7, Parny — Evariste-Désiré de Parny (1753–1814), French author of elegant amorous, mock-epic and neoclassical verse. He had a very strong influence on Pushkin during his lyceum period.

p. 45

Vera Ivanova-Shvarsalon (1890–1920), daughter of the writer L.D. Zinovyeva-Annibal, stepdaughter and later the wife of the Symbolist poet Vyacheslav Ivanov.

pp. 47-49

Although written contemporaneously with the other poems of *Evening,* these poems were not published as part of the first edition.

p. 53

In a manuscript version, this poem has the title "The Stray Dog." It first appeared in *Apollon*, No. 3 (1913), p. 36 under the title "Cabaret Artistique."

This poem is set in the cabaret called the Stray Dog, where Akhmatova often recited her poems in the early, spectacular years of her success. The Stray Dog, a meeting place for poets, painters, artists and bohemians, was in a cellar of house #5 on Mikhailovsky Square (now *Ploshchad iskusstv,* Art Square) in Petersburg. It existed from December 1911 to the spring of 1915. Its walls were painted by artist and set designer Sergey Sudeikin. Here members of different poetic groups came together and sometimes clashed. Symbolist poems were recited. Akhmatova, Gumilyov, and Mandelstam recited their Acmeist works, and Mayakovsky came from Moscow and shocked the Petersburg public with his Futurist poems. In her memoirs, Akhmatova recalls "the gate which we entered in order to descend the winding cellar staircase into the multicolored, smoky, always somewhat mysterious Stray Dog."

Line 15

"that woman dancing" — This woman was Olga Glebova-Sudeikina (1885–1945), dramatic actress, singer and dancer, wife of Sergey Sudeikin, and a close friend of Akhmatova, who frequently watched Sudeikina perform on the Stray Dog's small stage. Akhmatova lived with her from 1921–24 after the break-up of her marriage to Shileiko. Glebova-Sudeikina emigrated to Paris in 1924. In the role of the "Colombine of the 1910s" she is, as the double of Akhmatova, one of the main characters in *Poem Without a Hero.*

The tone of despair in this poem was caused by the recent suicide of Vsevolod Knyazev, a young poet and Officer of the Guard who was in love with Sudeikina. Knyazev's suicide, which involved Sudeikina, was the catalyst for Akhmatova's longest poem, *Poem Without a Hero.*

p. 73

N.V.N. — Nikolay Vladimirovich Nedobrovo. This poem seems to be a response to Nedobrovo's article about her poetry.

p. 79

Line 15, "her white mantle" — a reference to the legend that the Mother of God appeared in a church in Constantinople in the tenth century. According to the legend, the Madonna materialized in the center of the church and extended her veil over the people. The holiday celebrating this event, Pokrov, was very popular in Russia and symbolized the Madonna as intercessor for the people.

p. 83

Germany declared war on Russia on 1 August (19 July Old Style) 1914.

p. 89

Line 8, "Jonah's Monastery" — the Jonah Trinity Monastery, Kiev. Akhmatova went to Kiev to see her family on 17 May after she had gone with Gumilyov to northern Italy.

p. 101

The poem is titled "To My Fellow Citizens" in the 1923 edition of *Anno Domini*. The page was torn out by the Soviet censor from almost every copy of the edition. Several copies of this edition have by chance been preserved.

Petrograd — The city of Petersburg became Petrograd during World War I. Petersburg sounded too Germanic to patriotic Russians, and the old Slavic word for city, *grad*, was used to name "Peter's city." After Lenin's death in 1924 the name of the city was changed to Leningrad." The name of St. Petersburg was restored by a referendum of 1991.

p. 105

In the autumn of 1918, Akhmatova moved with Shileiko to Moscow, to 3 Zatchatevsky Street, near the present Kropotkin Street, where they lived until January 1919. Then, they moved back to Petrograd to the Marble Palace, where Shileiko had two rooms, as an employee of the Academy of Material Culture.

p. 115

When this poem was first published, it appeared without the fourth stanza. Gumilyov was executed on 25 August 1921.

p. 121

Line 7, Sheremetev lindens — in the garden of the Sheremetev Palace (Fountain House), where Akhmatova lived most of her adult life, from 1926 to 1941 and from 1944 to 1952 in the communal Punin apartment.

p. 123

The Poet — Boris Pasternak (1890–1960), poet, novelist and translator whose novel, *Dr. Zhivago,* was rejected for publication in the Soviet Union, and subsequently published in the West, following which Pasternak was awarded the Nobel Prize for Literature in 1958. He was, however, forced to refuse the award. The poem is constructed on Pasternakian motifs.

Line 15 — The Daryal Gorge runs through the Caucasus into Georgia. In the '30s, Pasternak visited the Georgian poets Paolo Yashvili and Titsian Tabidze, both of whom perished in the purges.

p. 127

O.M. — Osip Mandelstam (1891–1938), one of Russia's leading poets, who was closely associated with Akhmatova from the time of their membership in the Poets' Guild. Akhmatova was present when Mandelstam was first arrested for having written an anti-Stalin poem. She later visited him and his wife Nadezhda in Voronezh in 1936, where they were living in exile.

Line 5, Peter of Voronezh — a statue of Peter the Great

Line 8, Battle of Kulikovo — fought in 1380 near Voronezh. Dmitry Donskoy defeated one of the claimants to the throne of the Golden Horde, the Mongolians dominating Russia. Although the Mongols avenged the defeat by sacking Moscow two years later, the Battle of Kulikovo proved that the Russians could fight their Tatar overlords successfully. When this poem was first published, in the journal *Leningrad* in 1940, the last four lines were omitted.

pp. 131-151 REQUIEM

According to Lydia Chukovskaya, *Requiem* was memorized by people whom Akhmatova trusted, ten in all. The manuscripts as a rule were burned. Only in 1962 did Akhmatova give *Requiem* to the journal *Novy Mir*, but they rejected it. By this time *samizdat* (underground) copies were circulating widely. One of the copies made its way abroad and was published in Munich, 1963.

Instead of a Preface

Nadezhda Mandelstam writes, in *Hope Abandoned,* that "Stalin's Great Purge reached its height under the direction of Nikolay Yezhov (1894–1939), chief of the NKVD [the secret police] from 1936–38. He was then made the scapegoat for its 'excesses.' He was succeeded by Beria in 1938, and was probably executed in 1939, although there has never been any official information about his fate."

Akhmatova's son Lev Gumilyov was first arrested in 1933 on trumped-up charges, but was released nine days later. In October 1935 he was arrested again along with Punin. After Akhmatova wrote a letter to Stalin, they were both released in November 1935. Lev was arrested again in March 1938 and sentenced to ten years in the camps. The case was reviewed, and the sentence was changed to five years. He was released during World War II to fight against the Germans and participated in the taking of Berlin. He was arrested again in 1949 and released only in 1956 under a general amnesty following Stalin's death. In 1975, he was "rehabilitated" and declared innocent. Punin was also arrested in 1949 and sent to a Siberian camp, where he died in 1953.

Akhmatova, whose son was in prison, waited in line with others hoping to learn something about the fate of their relatives.

Dedication

Line 4, "prisoners' burrows" — from Pushkin's poem, "Message to Siberia."

Poem I

Line 1, "They led you away at dawn" — This poem refers to the arrest of Nikolay Punin (1888–1953), the art historian and critic with whom Akhmatova lived from 1926 until the late Thirties. After the Revolution, he worked under Lunacharsky in the Fine Arts section of the People's Commissariat of Enlightenment. During the purges Punin was arrested and sent to a forced-labor camp. He died in a camp in Abez, Siberia in August 1953.

Line 7, the Streltsy — an elite military corps instituted by Ivan the Terrible. Their mutiny in 1698 was mercilessly crushed by Peter the Great and 2,422 of them were tortured and hanged. Their wives pleaded for them "under the Kremlin towers." This incident is the subject of Vasily Surikov's painting, "The Morning of the Execution of the Streltsy."

Poem II

Line 1, "Quietly flows the quiet Don" — By using the name of a river in another part of Russia, Akhmatova expands the poem to include the suffering of all Russia.

Line 7, "Husband in the grave" — refers to Gumilyov who was executed on 25 August 1921.

Poem IV

Line 6, Kresty prison — A notorious political prison in Leningrad built in the configuration of crosses.

Poem V

Last line, "enormous star" — James H. Billington, in *The Icon and the Axe,* p. 383, points out that in Dostoevsky's *The Idiot,* the Christ figure, Prince Myshkin, returns to Russia and sees in the railroads the configuration of the great star Wormwood, which falls upon "the third part of the rivers and the fountains of the waters" causing great destruction and loss of life (Book of Revelation 8:10–12). In the same chapter of Revelation there is mention of a censer and foliage being destroyed, and in 9:7–11, there is a description of beings part beast, part insect, part human who torment people for a fixed number of months. All of these apocalyptical events have parallels in this short poem.

Poem VI

Line 3, white nights — In the summer in St. Petersburg night brings only a few hours of dusk.

Poem VII

This poem is dated the day of Lev Gumilyov's sentence to labor camp (Anna Akhmatova, *Selected Poems,* trans. Richard McKane [Bloodaxe Books, 1989], note, p. 332).

Poem VIII

Line 11, "the top of a pale blue cap" — a reference to the blue caps of the NKVD (the secret police)

Line 13, Yenisey — The Yenisey river in Siberia was the location of many of the concentration/labor camps.

Poem X

Epigraph — These lines, from the 9th chant of the Holy Week service, are inexactly quoted by Akhmatova. The correct quotation is, "Do not weep for Me, Mother,/ As you gaze upon the tomb."

Line 4, "Why hast Thou forsaken me?" — the last words of Christ (Matthew 27:46)

Epilogue II

Line 1, Remembrance Day — A memorial service is held on the anniversary of the death of a member of the Russian Orthodox church.

Line 23, "cherished pine stump" — a reference to Akhmatova's youthful strolls in the Tsarskoye Selo park, where Pushkin had also strolled.

p. 153

Epigraph — from Pushkin's poem, "Cleopatra"

Line 2, Augustus — The Roman Emperor Augustus (Octavius, 63 B.C.–14 A.D.) was victorious over his rival Antony, captured Egypt (where Antony had fallen in love with Cleopatra) and had the intention of taking Cleopatra and her children to Rome as prisoners in his triumphal procession. This poem was written while Akhmatova's son, Lev Gumilyov, was in prison.

p. 155

Epigraph — The citation from Dante's *Inferno,* Canto XIX, line 17, is slightly inaccurate. "...del mio bel San Giovanni" ("of my beautiful San Giovanni"), the Baptistry of the Florence Cathedral. The canto concerns the sin of simony, the buying and selling of ecclesiastical preferment or pardons, and describes the torments of the medieval popes in hell. Written the same year as "Voronezh," this poem may refer to Mandelstam's exile as well as Dante's.

Lines 10–11, "With a lighted candle he did not walk..." — Dante Aligheri (1265–1321) was not only a poet but also an active political figure in Florence. He was exiled from his native city in 1302 after the victory of the opposing party. In 1315 Dante was offered a proposal to return to Florence under conditions of humiliating public repentance which he decisively rejected. These lines refer to the ceremony of repentance. (Allusion provided by Prof. Pamela Davison in her paper on Dante and Akhmatova presented at the Akhmatova Centennial Conference at the University of Nottingham, England, July 1989.)

p. 159

This poem was written by Akhmatova to mark the 10th anniversary of Vladimir Mayakovsky's death. She was invited to recite it at the Leningrad Academy Chapel on 14 April 1940 in memory of Mayakovsky.

p. 167

Published first in *Leningrad,* No. 1–2, 1946, "To the Memory of a Friend" is another in the group of Akhmatova's poems that Zhdanov condemned in his decree of 14 August 1946; the journal was suppressed.

p. 171

First published in *Leningrad,* No. 1–2, 1946, this poem is another in the group condemned by Zhdanov in his decree of 14 August 1946.

pp. 175-179

Poems inspired by the unexpected visit of the British intellectual Isaiah Berlin (b. 1909) to Akhmatova at Fountain House, autumn 1945. According to Anatoly Naiman (*Rasskazy o Anne Akhmatovoi* [Moscow: Khudozhestvennaya literatura, 1989], published in English as *Remembering Anna Akhmatova,* trans. Wendy Rosslyn [New York: Henry Holt, 1991], p. 97), "From 1945 onwards, her (Akhmatova's) 'distant love' for the lover (Anrep) who had sailed away to London was connected, intertwined with, and, on the literary plane, enriched by, her feelings for another Russian who had also emigrated from Petersburg — but as a boy with his family, first to Latvia and then to England." This man was Isaiah Berlin. He came to see her again on 5 January 1946, on his way back to England.

Epigraph — concluding lines of Baudelaire's poem "Une Martyre"

p. 179

Line 5, "burnt drama" — a play written by Akhmatova in her Tashkent years. Fragments of it survive as *Prologue.* See pp. 535–539.

pp. 181-185

These poems also have references to the meeting with Isaiah Berlin. Berlin telephoned her when he visited the Soviet Union again in 1956. They did not meet because Akhmatova was afraid this would affect the fate of her son, who had just been released from prison.

p. 181

Nadezhda Mandelstam says about "Burnt Notebook":

The Tashkent *Prologue* was burned together with a notebook full of verse. Akhmatova made allusion to this in her poem, "The Burnt Notebook." When her volume of poetry was being put together, Surkov [Secretary of the Union of Soviet Writers, 1954–59] winced at this title: what did she mean by hinting that people had to burn their verse?... For propriety's sake he suggested she change it to "Notebook Lost in a Fire." Akhmatova duly made the change in her own hand, saying: "Very well, let people think I had a fire..." (Nadezhda Mandelstam, *Hope Abandoned* [Atheneum, 1974], p. 359)

Line 11, "the most sacred springtime" — the time in the poet's youth when she became aware of her poetic gift.

p. 185

Line 5, "For awhile you were my Aeneas" — As narrated in Virgil's *Aeneid,* Aeneas, fleeing from Troy, was hospitably received in the Carthaginian kingdom of Dido; he became her lover. But obeying the oracle, he had to abandon her in order to sail to Italy and found the city of Rome. The abandoned Dido immolated herself.

p. 193

Line 9, "mud on galoshes" — The expression may relate to the essay, "The Power of the Earth," by Gleb Uspensky (1843–1902): "The earth, in its unlimited, mighty power over the people, is not some kind of allegory or abstraction, but that very earth which you brought in from the street *on your galoshes in the form of dirt,* that same earth which lies in pots of flowers, the black, damp earth —in a word, the most ordinary and natural earth."

p. 195

Written for Joseph Brodsky, this is one of three poems written to her protégés Dmitry Bobyshev, Brodsky, and Anatoly Naiman that Akhmatova called the "rose cycle."

Epigraph — The epigraph, which does not appear in the Zhirmunsky edition, is from a poem dedicated to Akhmatova, "The cocks start crowing...," by Joseph Brodsky, who had written this poem for her birthday. (Brodsky realized her hopes by winning the Nobel Prize for Literature in 1987.) Akhmatova put the initials "I.B." [Iosif Brodsky] under the epigraph. At that time, Brodsky was almost totally unknown to the public. Readers searched for the line in the works of Ivan Bunin. Someone mentioned the "Guest from the Future," Isaiah Berlin. (See Anatoly Naiman, "Four Poems," in *Svoyu mezh vas yeshchyo ostaviv ten...*, Vol. III of *Akhmatova chteniya [Akhmatova Reader],* ed. N.V. Koroleva and S.A. Kovalenko [Moscow: Naslediye, 1992], p. 53.) After Akhmatova's poem was published in *Novy mir,* No. 1 (1963), the epigraph did not appear for over a quarter of a century in the Soviet Union because of the political scandal the government instigated around Brodsky.

Dmitry Bobyshev once brought Akhmatova a bouquet of roses. According to Kralin, she told him that all soon faded but one, which produced a "miracle" — the poem "The Fifth Rose," dedicated to Bobyshev. According to Naiman, she intended "The Last Rose," "The Fifth Rose," and "You — in fact..." (written to Naiman) to form a "rose cycle." (See Naiman, "Four Poems," p. 53.)

Line 1, Morozova — Feodosiya Morozova (d. 1675), an adherent of the archpriest Avvakum in the 17th century schism between the Patriarch Nikon and Avvakum. Nikon pressed for innovations in the Orthodox Church, but Morosova, a noblewoman, made no attempt to hide her affinity with the schismatics, the "Old Believers," as they were called. Avvakum was burned at the stake and in November 1672 Morozova was arrested, confined to a Moscow convent and tortured on the rack. She was subsequently incarcerated in a pit in the small town of Borovsk, where she died in 1675.

p. 197

Valeriya Sreznevskaya — This poem was written on the day of her death.

pp. 199-219 THE NORTHERN ELEGIES

The history of the creation of the *Northern Elegies* has been related in the manuscript Preface to the fragmentary "Seventh Elegy" (Central State Archive of Literature and Art, Moscow): "Soon after the end of the war I wrote two long poems in blank verse [apparently, 'I, like a river...' and 'There are three ages to memories...'] and christened them 'Leningrad elegies.' Then I joined two more poems to them ['Dostoevsky's Russia' and 'It was dreadful to live in that house']. The rest — seven of them were conceived — lived in me in different stages of readiness. One, especially ('The Seventh'), was thought out up to the end and, as always, something was noted down, something lost, something forgotten, something recalled, when suddenly it turned out that I loved them for their unanimity, for their total readiness to condemn me for anything they pleased."

The fragmentary "Seventh Elegy" was published in *Ya — golos vash... (I — Am Your Voice...)*, Moscow, 1989. The even more fragmentary "Lyrical Digression on the Seventh Elegy" was published in Anna Akhmatova, *Works* (Moscow, 1990), edited by M.M. Kralin. Kralin's compilation of the *Northern Elegies* opens with four lines from the Akhmatova file, Manuscript Department of the National Library of Russia, St. Petersburg (formerly Saltykov-Shchedrin State Public Library — GPB). Kralin presents the elegies in a different order than Zhirmunsky, whose order is based upon that of *The Flight of Time*. Although we follow Zhirmunsky's order, we have added epigraphs published by Kralin for the Third, Fourth, and Fifth elegies, and a dedication to the Fifth.

p. 199

Epigraph — an imprecise citation from Pushkin's "House in Kolomna." In Pushkin it reads: "I live there no longer." See A.S. Pushkin, "Domik v Kolomne," *Izbrannye proizvedeniya* [Moscow and Leningrad: Gosudarstvennoe izdatelstvo detskoi literatury, 1949], II, p. 285.

In her unfinished memoirs, in the manuscript section (GPB), Akhmatova describes Petersburg in these words: "The first (lower) layer for me is the Petersburg of the '90s, the Petersburg of Dostoevsky. It was dressed from head to foot in tasteless signboards — underwear, corsets, hats, without any greenery, without grass, without flowers; drums were beating continuously, thus always recalling capital punishment; French was spoken and there were grandiose funeral processions along the thoroughfares described by Mandelstam."

Line 4, Gorokhovaya (street) — was the main street of the merchants of 19th century St. Petersburg, as Nevsky Prospekt was the principal street for the aristocracy. After the Revolution, the corner building on Gorokhovaya (No. 1 or No. 2) became the headquarters of the Cheka, or secret police. Later, it was renamed after the first head of the Cheka, Felix Dzerzhinsky; it has now returned to its prerevolutionary name.

Line 18, "the Moderne" — Stile Moderne or Art Nouveau, a style at the turn of the century based on organic forms. Its typical motif is an undulant line usually with tile decorations on the façade. At the beginning of the 20th century several houses were built in the Stile Moderne on the odd-numbered side of Liteiny Prospekt.

Line 19, Nekrasov — Nikolay Nekrasov (1821–78), poet, editor, and publisher. In 1846 he acquired *Sovremennik,* which became the best literary and progressive journal of the day. Nekrasov is knowfor his poetry describing the plight of workers and peasants. The later generation of Symbolists thought his poetry too politically engaged to be great art. However, he had a strong impact on Akhmatova's work, and was one of the poets whom her mother read to her as a child.

Line 20, Saltykov — Mikhail Saltykov (1826–89), satirical novelist whose works are directed against the bureaucracy, the petty officials and the faults and foibles of the landed and middle classes

pp. 199-203 FIRST

Line 23, Old Russa — refers to Staraya Russa, a town between Moscow and St. Petersburg, in the region of the Valday highlands, which was the setting for Dostoevsky's novel, *The Brothers Karamazov.* Dostoevsky mainly spent the summers in Staraya Russa but also passed the winter of 1874–75 there. See Anna Dostoevsky, *Dostoevsky: Reminiscenses*, trans. Beatrice Stillman (New York: Liveright, 1975), p. 238.

Line 30, Optina — location (Kozelsky district) of a monastery that became a great place of pilgrimage. Tolstoy and Dostoevsky as well as many other members of the intelligentsia visited it in the nineteenth century. Here Dostoevsky met the monk Ambrose, who served as the prototype for the Elder Zosima in *The Brothers Karamazov.*

Line 40, Baden — Baden-Baden was a fashionable spa in Germany where Dostoevsky gambled.

Line 41, "a woman" — Inna Gorenko (ca. 1852–1930)

pp. 203-205 SECOND

Line 18, "The queen of the sea" — an allusion to Lermontov's poem, "The Queen of the Sea." See *Zh. 650,* lines 5 & 6 (in *Poem Without a Hero* section, p. 583) and note.

Line 25, "Fifteen years ago" — Akhmatova went to live with art historian and critic Nikolay Punin in his apartment in Fountain House in 1926. His wife and daughter shared the same flat. Akhmatova and Punin finally separated in 1938. She continued to live in the communal Punin apartment in her own room.

Last line, "stand in splendor" — The Russian verb refers to a custom practiced at folk weddings. The bride parades back and forth before friends and relatives so they can admire her headdress and other finery.

pp. 205-207 THIRD

Epigraph — from Tyutchev's poem, "Cicero"

N.A.O. — Nina Antonovna Olshevskaya, a close friend of Akhmatova's. Akhmatova often stayed at her home in Moscow.

Line 21, "some other woman" — Anna Engelhardt, second wife of Gumilyov.

The more complete, Struve-Filippov version of this poem appears here. This includes lines 27–36, which, in the Zhirmunsky edition, appear in the Notes and Variants section rather than in the main text.

pp. 209-211 FOURTH

Epigraph — from Pushkin's poem, "Three Keys"

Line 43, "That everything turned out for the best..." — a phrase relating to Voltaire's *Candide*, cited by Alexander Radishchev, an 18th century writer who decried the evils of serfdom, in one of his letters written in French, which Akhmatova translated at the end of the 1940s. Voltaire's work is a satire on the philosophical view that no matter how deplorable our condition, "Everything is for the best."

pp. 211-213 FIFTH

Line 14, Proserpina — ancient goddess, daughter of Demeter, who, according to legend, was abducted by the god Pluto, ruler of the Underworld. During springtime Proserpina returns to earth and dances with her friends in a meadow.

p. 215 SIXTH

The more complete, Struve-Filippov version of this poem appears here. This includes lines 6–8, which, in the Zhirmunsky edition, appear in the Notes and Variants section but not in the main text.

Line 1, "that house" — Akhmatova and Gumilyov were married in 1910. They lived in Gumilyov's mother's house, on Malaya 63, in Tsarskoye Selo.

pp. 217-219 SEVENTH

The unfinished Seventh *Northern Elegy* was published in substantial portion for the first time, to our knowledge, in Chernykh, ed., *Ya — golos vash... (I — Am Your Voice...),* Moscow: Knizhnaya palata, 1989.

p. 221

Line 2, *Figaro* — a Parisian newspaper that reviews books and cultural events. Akhmatova was in Paris in the spring of 1910 and 1911.

p. 225

This demonic portrait of Blok foreshadows the later stanzas about him in *Poem Without a Hero.*

p. 231

In one of Akhmatova's tables of contents (TsGALI) the poem is titled "To the Memory of Yesenin," and in the manuscript of "Odd" (GPB), "In Memory of Sergey Yesenin," with the date 1925. The fact that the poem was written before Yesenin's (1895–1925) death is confirmed in a note in Pavel Luknitsky's diary: "A.A. read this poem on 25 February 1925 in the hall of the State Academy Chapel (Moika, 20) at a large literary evening of contemporary poetry and prose." (Luknitsky archive) Yesenin committed suicide on 27 December 1925.

p. 235

The source of this poem is a work by Hovaness Toumanian (1869–1923). In the original, the poet has a dream that he is the ruler and a black ewe approaches him. In Akhmatova's poem the poetess is a black ewe and approaches the ruler in his dreams. A second possible source suggested by Kralin is a medieval Armenian fable from the collection by Vartan Aigektsi, *The Prince and the Widow*, printed in translation in the journal *Zvezda*, No. 3, 1937. Akhmatova might have known the fable and the quatrain by Toumanian in the paraphrase of Mandelstam.

"Imitation from the Armenian," with its obvious reference to Stalin, has often been published abroad. It was published in the Soviet magazine *Radio and Television* in 1966.

p. 237

Mikhail Bulgakov — Novelist, author of the *The Master and Margarita*, which was published in 1966, 26 years after his death.

p. 239

Epigraph — from a poem of Marina Tsvetaeva's entitled "To Akhmatova" (1921). In 1916 Tsvetaeva had devoted a large cycle of poems to Akhmatova, but had received no reply at that time.

Line 5, Marinkina Tower — in the Kolomna Kremlin, where, according to legend, Marina Mnishek was imprisoned. Mnishek was the Polish noblewoman who became the wife of the monk Otryopov.

p. 241

De Profundis — "From the depths," the beginning of the Roman Catholic prayer for the dead.

p. 243

Epigraph — Innokenty Basalaev (1897–1964), a writer, literary scholar, editor, and second husband of the poet Ida Nappelbaum (daughter of the famous photographer Moses Nappelbaum). Basalaev came to Leningrad from Tashkent.

Line 6, Beshagach — a square in Tashkent

Line 13, *Rakhmat* — "thank you" in Uzbek

Khaier — "goodbye" in Uzbek

Chusti — Uzbek poet

Line 15, Aibek — the real name of Musa Tashmukhamedov (1905–68), Uzbek writer

Line 16, Toshkent — Uzbek pronunciation of Tashkent

Line 19, *baranchuks* — "little boys" in Uzbek.

p. 261

Bachianas Brasileiras — by Hector Villa-Lobos. Akhmatova wrote about this poem: "Last evening I was listening to the *Bachianas Brasileiras*, sung by Galina Vishnevskaya. I composed something, but in the darkness I couldn't write it down and it seems I forgot it."

Notes to "Mirrors and Masks"

[1]Natalya Ilina, "Anna Akhmatova v poslednie gody ee zhizni," *Oktyabr*, No. 2 (1977), p. 123.

[2]Anna Akhmatova, "Korotko o sebe" in Anna Akhmatova, *Stikhotvoreniya i poemy*, ed. V.M. Zhirmunsky, Biblioteka poeta, Bolshaya seriya, 2nd ed. (Leningrad: Sovetskii pisatel, 1979), p. 22.

[3]See Richard Charques, *The Twilight of Imperial Russia* (London: Oxford University Press, 1958).

[4]Midsummer Eve, June 23rd, is known in Russian folklore as "The Eve of Ivan Kupala." The holiday reflects a double belief system — pagan and Christian — as it is the eve of the celebration of both St. John the Baptist and the spirit "Kupala," the "Bather." People bathed in rivers and lakes and jumped through bonfires for purification. Satan calls his followers to a feast on Bald Mountain in the Ukraine. Akhmatova knew these customs and the significance of the date for the Russian people. For a description of the rituals and songs sung on this night, see *The Russian Folk Lyric*, trans. and ed. Roberta Reeder (Bloomington: Indiana University Press, 1992), pp. 84–86.

[5]Akhmatova's father, Andrey Gorenko, was born in Sevastopol on 13 January 1848, and served as an engineer in the Black Sea Fleet. His father had also been in the navy, and received two high awards for his service, thereby acquiring hereditary nobility. Gorenko was appointed instructor at the naval institute in Petersburg in 1875, but in 1880, some letters of his that were deemed "suspicious" were found in the apartment of a friend. In September 1881, he was relieved of his position as instructor and put under surveillance. His sisters, Anna and Evgeniya, who had attended the Bestuzhev Women's Courses in Petersburg, were also under surveillance for their work in the radical "People's Will" movement. By October 1882, lack of evidence enabled him to return to the Black Sea Fleet. He married Inna Stogova, Akhmatova's mother, in 1885, and their first daughter, Iya, was born that same year.

Gorenko retired with a pension in 1887 with the rank of captain, and he and his family settled in Odessa. He worked on the newspaper, *Odesskie novosti*, writing reviews of literature — the memoirs of Garibaldi, novels of Daudier — and published a novella, *The Philosopher Sikundus*, and a short story.

In August 1890, Gorenko and his family moved to Tsarskoye Selo. In 1905 he left his family to live with E.I. Stranoliubskaya, widow of a friend with whom he had taught at the naval institute. He died on 25 August 1915 at the age of 67. See Roman Shuvalov, "Otets poeta. K 100-letiyu so dnya rozhdeniya Anny Akhmatovoi," *Vechernyaya Odessa*, 14 June 1989, p. 3.

[6]Vitaly Vilenkin mentions that Akhmatova's mother, Inna Stogova, had become involved with one of the most radical political groups in Russia, the "People's Will." See Vilenkin, *V sto pervom zerkale* (Moscow: Sovetskii pisatel, 1987), p. 89. Akhmatova notes in a reminiscence entitled "Gorod" that when her mother visited her for the last time in 1927, she was full of memories of the People's Will and recalled the Petersburg of her youth in the 1870s.

Akhmatova's mother died in 1930. See Akhmatova, *Ya — golos vash...*, ed. V.A. Chernykh (Moscow: Knizhnaya palata, 1989), p. 340. Akhmatova told her friend Lidiya Chukovskaya that her mother came from nobility but attended courses in her youth, which was unusual for women gentry of the time. See Chukovskaya, *Zapiski ob Anne Akhmatovoi*, Vol. I, 1938–1941 (Paris: YMCA Press, 1976), p. 181.

[7]Akhmatova writes in her memoir "Budka" (Akhmatova, *Ya — golos vash...*, p. 337) that she was named after her maternal grandmother, Anna Motovilov. Her pseudonym, Akhmatova, is based on the maiden name of her great-grandmother, Praskovya, who came from a family of Simbirsk gentry, the Akhmatovs. According to family legend, the Akhmatovs descended from Akhmat, the last of the great Tatar khans who ruled Russia, and who died in 1481. Akhmatova says this great-grandmother was also a Genghizid — a descendent of Genghis Khan. She notes that Khan Akhmat was killed by a paid assassin, and his death symbolized the end of the Mongol yoke in Russia. See Charles J. Halperin, *Russia and the Golden Horde* (Bloomington: Indiana University Press, 1987) for a discussion of the Mongol invasion and the episode concerning Akhmat.

Akhmatova's mother's father descended from the Stogovs, landowners from the Moscow province who moved there when Novgorod came under siege by Ivan III in the 15th century.

[8]Chukovskaya, I, p. 81.

[9]Akhmatova, *Stikhi, perepiska, vospominaniya, ikonografiya*, comp. E. Proffer (Ann Arbor: Ardis, 1977), p. 96.

[10]V.S. Sreznevskaya, "Iz vospominanii V.S. Sreznevskoi," in N. Gumilyov, *Neiz-dannoe i nesobrannoe*, comp. and ed. Michael Basker and Sheelagh Duffin Graham (Paris: YMCA Press, 1986), p. 160.

[11]Earl D. Sampson, *Nikolay Gumilev* (Boston: Twayne Publishers, 1979), p. 48, states the essential themes of Gumilyov's work: search for the ideal, the struggle of the individualist as poet, prophet, aesthete, and "conquistador."

[12]Gleb Struve, "N.S. Gumilyov: Zhizni i lichnost," in Gumilyov, *Sobranie sochinenii*, I, p. xii. Sampson notes the conflicting testimony regarding the number and dates of Gumilyov's trips to Africa. See Sampson, *op. cit.*, p. 24.

[13]Akhmatova, "Korotko o sebe," p. 20.

[14]It was Russia's Silver Age which was marked by great writers but also com-posers such as Alexander Scriabin, Rimsky-Korsakov, and Tchaikovsky, as well as artists such as Mikhail Vrubel. The Golden Age was that of Pushkin in the early 19th century.

[15]Chukovskaya, I, p. 158.

[16]Irina Graham as cited by Mikhail Kralin in *Artur i Anna* (Leningrad: M.M. Kralin, 1990).

[17]Amanda Haight, *Anna Akhmatova: A Poetic Pilgrimage* (New York and London: Oxford University Press, 1976), p. 18.

[18]Mikhail Kuzmin, "Predislovie M.A. Kuzmina k pervoi knige stikhov Anny Akhmatovoi" in Anna Akhmatova, *Sochineniya*, ed. G.P. Struve and B.A. Filippov, Vol. III (Paris: YMCA Press, 1983), pp. 471–473.

[19]Korney Chukovsky, *Lyudi i knigi*, Vol. V (Moscow: Khudozhestvennaya literatura, 1960), p. 754.

[20]Amanda Haight, "Letters from Nikolay Gumilyov to Anna Akhmatova, 1912–1915," *Slavonic and Eastern European Review*, Vol. L, No. 118 (1972) p. 101. That same year, 1912, Gumilyov had an affair with Olga Vysotskaya, who gave birth to their son in October 1913. Anatoly Naiman writes that in the early 1960s Akhmatova called Olga Vysotskaya to come over to confirm some fact from the 1910s. He and Boris Ardov brought Vysotskaya by taxi to the Ardovs where Akhmatova was staying. Akhmatova sat with her hair carefully combed, wearing lipstick and a pretty dress, surrounded by admirers, with her one-time rival — a weak, old woman, broken by fate. (Anatoly Naiman, *Rasskazy o Anne Akhmatavoi* [Moscow: Khudozhestvennaya literatura, 1989], p. 221, published in English as *Remembering Anna Akhmatova*, trans. Wendy Rosslyn [New York: Henry Holt, 1991], p. 215.)

In the Appendix of Jessie Davies' biography, *Anna of all the Russias* (Liverpool: Lincoln Davies & Co., 1988), pp. 134–135, there is a translation of an interview with Orest Vysotsky that appeared in *Soviet Weekly*, 14 May 1988, p. 5, in which he says he and his mother got to know Akhmatova and Lev Gumilyov in 1936 in Leningrad. Orest went to see Lev in March on the evening of his arrest. Orest was also arrested at this time for "counter-revolutionary terrorist activity," and released after a year and a half.

[21]Sreznevskaya, in N. Gumilyov, *op. cit.*, p. 164.

[22]Vera Luknitskaya, *Pered toboi zemlya* (Leningrad: Lenizdat, 1988), p. 291.

[23]Sam Driver, *Anna Akhmatova* (New York: Twayne Publishers, 1972), p. 77. Akhmatova's view of Petersburg is similar to that of the World of Art Group. Major articles were written for their journal about Petersburg of the 18th century and during the time of Pushkin. They called this admiration for early Petersburg "Retrospectivism," which they considered part of the Russian revival movement that began in the last part of the 19th century. Muscovites in the group turned to famous medieval cities, but the Petersburg group turned to the art and architecture of their own city as equally important in reverence for Russia's past and its traditions.

[24]Haight, p. 10.

[25]V.M. Zhirmunsky, *Tvorchestvo Anny Akhmatovoi* (Leningrad: Nauka, 1973), p. 126.

[26]N.S. Nedobrovo, "Anna Akhmatova," *Russkaya mysl*, No. 17 (July 1915), pp. 50–68. A translation of this article appears in *Russian Literature Triquarterly*, No. 9 (Spring 1974), pp. 221–236.

[27]Haight, personal communication. Haight says Akhmatova told Anatoly Naiman that when Nedobrovo saw Anrep with her early in 1916, he realized that his friend had been able to evoke a response in her that he had never been able to win himself. Akhmatova said she felt guilty about this.

[28]For two interesting articles on Anrep in England during World War I, see Wendy Rosslyn, "A propos of Anna Akhmatova: Boris Vasilievich Anrep (1883–1969)," *New Zealand Slavonic Journal*, No. 1 (1980), pp. 25–34, and "Boris Anrep and the Poems of Anna Akhmatova," in *The Modern Language*

Review, Vol. 74, Pt. 4 (October 1979), pp. 884–896. In the latter article, Rosslyn cites Akhmatova's poem, "I, like a river…" *(S-F. III, 79–80)* from the *Northern Elegies* in which the poet points out other directions her life might have taken. Had she gone to England, she, like Anrep, might have become part of a circle that included the writer Aldous Huxley and the art critic Roger Fry.

[29]Chukovskaya, I, p. 161. Gumilyov married Anna Engelhart, the daughter of a professor of Oriental Studies, and they had a daughter in 1920. In January 1921 he was elected president of the Petersburg section of the All-Russian Union of Poets, and from the spring of 1921 lived in the House of Artists. See Nikolay Otsup, "N.S. Gumilyov," in Nikolay Gumilyov, *Izbrannoe*, ed. Nikolay Otsup (Paris: Librarie des cinq continents, 1959), p. 16.

[30]Luknitsky provides an extensive description and diagram of the apartment. See Vera Luknitskaya, "Iz dvukh tysyach strech (Acumania)," *Pered toboi zemlya* (Leningrad: Lenizdat, 1988), p. 294 and p. 315. For an English translation, see Davies, *op. cit.*, pp. 43–44.

[31]Naiman, *op. cit.*, p. 79.

[32]Elaine Moch-Bickert, *Olga Glebova-Sudeikina* (Paris: Service de reproduction des thèses université de Lille, 1972), p. 56. For a Russian version of this book, see *Kolombina desyatykh godov…*, trans. Vera Rumyantseva, ed. Yu. A. Molok (Paris and St. Petersburg: Grzhebina-AO "Arsis," 1993).

[33]The NEP-man became a favorite target of satire. See Vladimir Mayakovsky's play, *The Bedbug* and his *poema*, *About This.*

[34]For a detailed account of the Tagantsev Affair, see Mikhail Heller and Aleksandr M. Nekrich, *Utopia in Power: The History of the Soviet Union from 1917 to the Present* (New York: Summit Books, 1986), pp. 139–140; and Roberta Reeder, *Anna Akhmatova: Poet and Prophet* (New York: St. Martin's Press, 1994), pp. 142–144.

[35]G.A. Terekhov, former assistant to the Procurator General of the U.S.S.R., wrote about his inquiry into Gumilyov's case in *Novy mir*, No. 12 (1987). He says that Gumilyov's complicity in a counterrevolutionary plot had not been confirmed by any documented evidence. His only guilt was a failure to report to the authorities an offer to join a clandestine organization. See Appendix to Davies, *op. cit.*, p. 134.

[36]Nikolay Gumilyov, "Zvezdnyi uzhas," *Sobranie sochinenii*, Vol. II, p. 63.

[37]Kuzmin wrote: "As soon as the suspicion of stagnation appears, the artist must plunge into the very depths of his soul and call forth a new source — or keep silent." Kuzmin, *Uslovnost. Stati ob iskusstve*. (Petrograd, 1923), p. 166, cited by Zhirmunsky, *Tvorchestvo*, p. 39.

[38]Haight, p. 80.

[39]Haight, pp. 81–82.

[40]Akhmatova would write a poem on a piece of paper, Chukovskaya would memorize it, and then Akhmatova would talk about the weather as she burned it in an ashtray. As early as the 1930s, Akhmatova feared her room might be bugged. (Chukovskaya, I, p. 162.)

[41]Lev Gumilyov, "'Inache poety net' (Beseda L.E. Varustina s L.N.

Gumilyovym)" *Zvezda*, No. 6 (1989), pp. 127–132.

[42]Chukovskaya, *Zapiski ob Anne Akhmatovoi*, Vol. I, 1938–1941 (St. Petersburg: Neva & Kharkov: Folio, 1996), p. 163. See the Introduction to *Reed* in the Notes to Poems section. Also, for more information on the history of Soviet censorship, see *Literary Front. History of Political Censorship 1932–1946* (Moscow: Entsiklopediya sovetskikh dereven, 1994).

[43]K.M. Azadovsky points out that poet Nikolay Klyuev once called Akhmatova "Kitezhanka." According to the legend, the city of Kitezh sank deep into a lake, where its towers can be seen on days when the water is especially clear. Klyuev had frequently turned to the theme of Kitezh, which seemed to him to embody the most cherished ideas about ancient, mysterious, "submerged" Russia, and which he believed would rise again in all its blinding beauty. By calling Akhmatova a "Kitezhanka," he suggested their common fate and spiritual kinship. See K.M. Azadovsky, "Menya nazval 'kitezhankoi': Anna Akhmatov i Nikolay Klyuev," *Literaturnoe obozrenie*, No. 5 (1989), p. 69. See the Notes to Poems, p. 833.

[44]For more information on the winter campaign against Finland, see Georg von Rauch, *A History of Soviet Russia*, ed. and trans. Peter and Annette Jacobsohn, 6th ed. (New York: Praeger Publishers, 1972), pp. 289–292.

[45]Akhmatova found Tashkent beautiful and exotic. Her sojourn there is reminiscent of the period Pushkin lived in exile in the south of Russia from 1820 to 1824. He wrote beautiful poems reflecting the cosmopolitan atmosphere, where Greeks, Serbs and Gypsies lived among the Ukrainian and Russian population. Still, Pushkin longed to be back in Petersburg with his friends.

[46]Haight, p. 122.

[47]Yu. I. Budyko, "Istoriya odnogo posvyashcheniya," *Russkaya literatura*, No. 1 (1984), p. 236. Aliger writes that Garshin's wife died in the winter of 1941. Margarita Aliger, "V poslednii raz," *Vospominaniya ob Anne Akhmatovoi*, ed. V.Y. Vilenkin and V.A. Chernykh (Moscow: Sovetskii pisatel, 1991), p. 349.

[48]Aliger, *Ibid.*, p. 349.

[49]N. Mandelstam, *Hope Abandoned*, p. 449.

[50]Emma Gershtein, "Nina Antonovna: Besedy ob Akhmatovoi s N.A. Olshevskoi-Ardovoi," *Literaturnoe obozrenie*, No. 5 (1989), p. 91.

[51]Aliger, *op. cit.*, p. 348.

[52]Personal communication with Nina Ivanovna Popova, Director of the Anna Akhmatova Museum, St. Petersburg.

[53]Haight, pp. 140–143.

[54]Haight, in a personal communication, notes that the Regulations against Akhmatova were published in numerous Soviet newspapers and journals. *Zvezda* was accused of popularizing Akhmatova's works and forced to change its editorial policy. *Leningrad* was suppressed. There was an unpleasant article on Akhmatova by I. Sergievsky ("About the Anti-National Poetry of Anna Akhmatova"), followed by another equally vile one by A. Volkov on the Acmeists ("Standard-bearers and Senselessness"), both in *Zvezda*. V.

Sidelnikov accused Akhmatova of being a traitor because she suggested Pushkin had taken the story of "The Golden Cockerel" from a foreign source ("Against Perversion and Obsequiousness in Soviet Folkloristics," *Literaturnaya gazeta*, No. 26 [2431] [Moscow, 29 June 1947], p. 3).

[55]In *Anna Akhmatova: Requiem*, ed. Roman Timenchik and K.M. Polivanov (Moscow: MPI, 1989), p. 231.

[56]Haight, p. 145.

[57]Punin's reputation has been restored in the Soviet Union. In their efforts to reflect a new enthusiasm for Russian avant-garde art, in 1988 the Soviets arranged an exhibit of art from the 1920s–30s at the New Tretyakov Gallery in Moscow. On 24 June 1988 a "Punin Evening" in Leningrad was dedicated to his memory, emphasizing the aesthetic discoveries of this period and his important contributions to them. The evening was sponsored by *Leningradnoe otdelenie sovetskogo funda kultury* (Leningrad section of the Soviet Cultural Fund), which also sponsored an evening devoted to Akhmatova in February, to Zoshchenko in April, and to Mandelstam in May of the same year.

[58]Haight, p. 175.

[59]Ilina, *op. cit.*, p. 129.

[60]Dmitry Bobyshev, "Akhmatovskie siroty," *Russkaya mysl*, No. 3507 (8 March 1984), pp. 8–9.

[61]Anna Akhmatova, *Sochineniya v dvukh tomakh*, ed. Mikhail Kralin, Vol. I (Moscow: Pravda, 1990), p. 426.

[62]See *S-F. I, 328–329 (Zh. 480); Zh. 590; Zh. 593* and notes.

[63]Anna Akhmatova, "Iz pisma k N." in Anna Akhmatova, *Sochineniya*, ed. Struve-Filippov, Vol. II (Munich: Inter-Language Literary Associates, 1968), p. 97.

[64]V.M. Zhirmunsky, "Anna Akhmatova i Aleksandr Blok," *Russkaya literatura*, No. 3 (1970), p. 77.

[65]Haight, p. 154.

[66]Raisa Orlova and Lev Kopelev provide Akhmatova's version of this visit. She was not allowed to receive Frost in her little cabin, so instead, went to the dacha of the academician Mikhail Alekseyev, which served as a "Potemkin village." The term derives from the period when Catherine the Great went to visit the Crimea to see the conquests of her lover, Grigory Potemkin. In order to impress her from afar, whole villages were painted on flats, which she saw from a distance. "Potemkin village" has come to mean a false façade.

[67]F.D. Reeve, *Robert Frost in Russia* (Boston: Little, Brown and Company, 1963), pp. 80–85.

[68]G.A. Adamovich, "Moi vstrechi s Annoi Akhmatovoi," *Vozdushnye puti* (1967), p. 107.

[69]*Ibid.*

[70]*Ibid.*, p. 114.

[71]Ironically, Akhmatova died on the anniversary of Stalin's death.

[72]R.D. Timenchik and A.V. Lavrov, "Materialy A.A. Akhmatovoi v rukopisnom otdele pushkinskogo doma," *Ezhegodnik rukopisnogo otdela pushkinskogo doma na 1974* (Leningrad: Nauka, 1976), p. 81.

[73]Nikita Struve, "Vosem chasov s Annoi Akhmatovoi," in Struve-Filippov, Vol. II, p. 346.

Judith Hemschemeyer began translating Anna Akhmatova's poems in 1976, and completed the first draft in 1981-82 with the assistance of a Hodder Fellowship from Princeton University. Hemschemeyer won the 1986 Associated Writing Programs (AWP) Poetry Prize for her collection, *The Ride Home*, which was published in 1987 by Texas Tech University Press. Wesleyan University Press published her two previous collections, *I Remember the Room Was Filled with Light* (1973) and *Very Close and Very Slow* (1975). Her translations of Akhmatova have appeared in many journals, including *The Hudson Review*, *Ploughshares*, *Calyx*, *Stand*, and *Northwest Review*, and have been reprinted widely in such books as *The Norton Anthology of World Masterpieces*, the *Bedford Introduction to Literature*, and *Love Poems. Everyman's Library Pocket Poets* (Alfred A. Knopf, 1993). She has also translated poems of Alexander Pushkin, Evgeny Rein, and Inna Lisnianskaya.

Roberta Reeder has been involved with Russian literature and culture for most of her life. She has taught at Harvard and Yale, and publishes articles, both here and abroad, on all aspects of Russian culture. She has contributed to or instigated events as diverse as a Ukrainian film festival, a drama based on Russian folk wedding traditions, and "The Russian Cabaret." The latter was a series of lecture-demonstrations based on the famous prerevolutionary cabarets — The Bat, the Poet's Cafe, and the Stray Dog. She has created a dramatization of Akhmatova's great poem, *Requiem*. In 1994, Reeder published *Anna Akhmatova: Poet and Prophet* (St. Martin's Press), which the late Stephen Spender called "more than just an excellent biography. It gives a vividly rich picture of the lives of the Russian intelligentsia throughout this century, and reveals so much about the land of Russia. A marvelous book." The paperback edition (1995) was named one of the best biographies of the year by the *N.Y. Times Book Review*.